Magical Multiple
MOMENTS

Parents of Multiples Share Stories and Advice
on Raising Happy, Healthy
Twins, Triplets, Quads, *and More!*

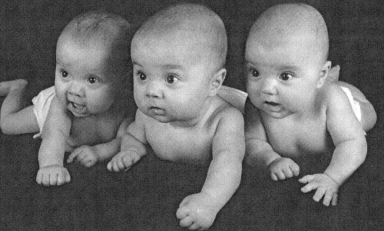

• • •

JULIE GILLESPIE

Magical Multiple Moments:
*Parents of Multiples Share Stories and Advice
on Raising Happy, Healthy
Twins, Triplets, Quads, and More!*

Julie Gillespie

Co-Editors: Rachel Fretz, Sandra Leer, Louise Spencer
Author Photo: Wendy Perl, perlphoto.com

ISBN: 978-1-936214-03-7

Library of Congress Control Number: 2009937857

Published by Orsi-Gillespie, an Imprint of Wyatt-MacKenzie

ORSI-GILLESPIE
an imprint of Wyatt-MacKenzie

www.wyattmackenzie.com

Magical Multiple
MOMENTS

TABLE OF CONTENTS

ACKNOWLEDGEMENTS

I want to take this opportunity to thank everyone who was involved in the process of writing this book.

Thank you to the Triplet Connection Magazine which inspired me to launch my voyage of writing my book, sharing ideas, and telling my personal story. Thanks also to the "Triplet Connection" website for advertising and finding volunteers for my multiples survey and to all the parents who participated in the survey and who lovingly shared their wisdom and ideas in the interviews. It takes a brave parent to tell the truth and the readers of this book will no doubt benefit from the breadth of their knowledge. I also wish to express my gratitude to my editors Rachel, Louise, Sandra, to my statistician Jiashen, to my data entry specialist Elise, and to my mother's helper Mirna. Without your help, this book would not have been possible.

Finally, and most importantly, thank you to my children, Tim, Alex, Jack, Sam, and Nicolas, and to my husband Bill who have put up with my "project" and been a consistent source of support, energy, and inspiration and who have taught me more about myself, my dogged determination, my ability to love and learn, and my sense of humor – thank you for being my greatest teachers.

A NOTE FROM THE AUTHOR

I wanted to add a note about what led me to write this book. Upon first discovering that we were pregnant I was overjoyed and filled with excitement. When we discovered we were pregnant with triplets a new set of emotions came to the forefront as I pondered what exactly it meant to parent multiples and how exactly these new bundles of joy would fit into our family. With nerves and trepidation, joy and excitement I carried our three little ones for 33 weeks and now raise them along side my teenage son and new baby.

This book represents a journey about learning, loving and laughing and about the trials and tribulations that I and other parents of multiples inevitably face in raising three or more little people all at the same time. I am better person for having had my children and a better parent for having written this book, and for that I am grateful. Life is a process that teaches us lessons from unexpected sources.

• • • • •

CHAPTER ONE

· · · · ·

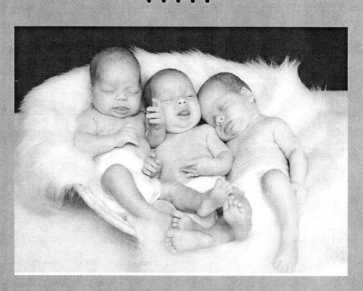

Introduction
Or
Captain's Log

Julie's Story
(Our story)

I was thirty-eight years old when we decided to seek assistance getting pregnant. At the time I was a doctor of physical therapy whose proudest moment was developing an independent clinical practice at USC. My husband Bill was working as a clinical psychiatrist. He had worked at UCLA for several years as a PhD molecular biologist. His claim to fame was a patent for cloning a segment of DNA.

We had been together for seven years and suddenly realized we had to get serious about having children together. We sought the help of fertility treatments after being unsuccessful on our own.

We did six rounds of IUI's (inter-uterine inseminations) and were unsuccessful. We were good candidates for IVF (in vitro fertilization) but were nervous about the possibility of multiples. We put our trust in the fertility doctors and nurses and we were not disappointed.

On the very first ultrasound I was excited to see two heart beats. "What's that shadow?" I asked Dr. Ringler at California Fertility Partners. "Oh, it's just a remaining egg sac, it will slough off.

Two weeks later, we went for a repeat ultrasound. This time Bill was able to join me. I don't remember looking at the ultrasound screen, I only remember the look on Bill's face as he fell back into the corner of the examination room, turned white as a ghost, and eased gently to the floor.

"Three?" Bill said. "How can there be three heart beats?" I don't remember what Dr. Ringler's response was I only remember how that moment in time changed forever what we thought were our greatest accomplishments were.

Suddenly we were launched on a journey we hadn't expected.

It's a sudden rush of fame…everyone at the fertility clinic knows you've hit the jack pot.

I felt somehow even more exceptional than "regular" parents who conceived via assisted fertility methods because it worked on our first IVF round plus I had been pregnant before. Our son was now in seventh grade.

When we started to tell our friends and family some were envious, some felt empathic, but they all had at least an opinion.

I tried to focus on what really mattered. A million questions came into my mind. Now that I have these "special babies", how will I go back to my routine life or do I? What can I do to make my singleton feel as special? How do I let my husband know that this new, completely more fulfilling life is going to make him significantly more strained financially? And how do I define who I am other then the "Triplets' Mom?"

Suddenly my son's seventh grade "Who Am I?" project comes running through my head. Not only do I have the constant question of "Who am I," but also, "What the heck am I going to do now? Return to work? Start my career over?"

Since I'm becoming such a celebrity now, will I be able to whip my body back into shape like Hiedi Klum or Jennifer Garner?

What I did for the first five years is in this book. Also, I've been privileged to include stories from other parents of multiplies. Not all parents of multiples started their journey as we did but many of us shared similar experiences. These pages will tell more about our joy.

Cheers!

· · ·

"I really feel that having multiples has shaped my life in a beautiful way. I believe I have met people I never would have met in any other way, learned more about myself and my many strengths. My children have NOT suffered. In my opinion, having triplets IS easier than three children two years apart for most of the time. I would like to see a book that cele-brates how different families succeed, not whine about how no one helps them."

Judie M., South Bend, Indiana

· · ·

My advice to new parents of multiples: "Slow down and 'Breathe'. I realized pretty quickly that I couldn't 'Do it all'. Even if you don't have outside help – it really helps to RE-prioritize. You realize that some of the small stuff (like having a spotless house) isn't really all that important anymore." When I asked Leslie if she would do anything differently, she replied: *"I would have relaxed and enjoyed ALL of my children more while they were little. I would have hugged more and worried about messes less. Listened more and lectured less.*

Leslie L., Dingle, Idaho
GGG 18 years old in 2008, G 20 years old, B 21 years old

• • •

I never dreamed I would have triplets, but three has always been my favorite number. I have three brothers, I have changed my name three times, and I have earned three degrees. Whenever I am asked to choose a number between one and ten, I always chose three. I had no idea how significant that number was going to be in my future. Now I look for books with three characters in them, stuffed animals in three varieties, outfits of matching trios, and three candy color-coded options. Is it some psychiatric syndrome, or do all parents of triplets suddenly look for sacred trinities?

I grew up in a home where all the cupboards were labeled, and every countertop was tidy. My mother had four children. She had to be organized. This is not the house I live in now. I have just one more child than my parents, yet "clutter" is no stranger in our house. My mother may have tried to pass down her organizational talents, but she did not have triplets. In fact, not one of the parents of multiples I've talked to in the past five years had parents who themselves had triplets. All of these interviewees and parents who filled out our surveys provided me with a "Mother-load" of information that couldn't be found in a book or in talking with friends or family.

My initial fear was that our three would always be lumped together as "The triplets" without respect for their individual personalities. When our three were born, we had a thirteen-year-old son. My parenting style had to change. Each one of our three could not have his/her own computer, laptop, car, or even his/her own room for that matter. Little did I know, my three wouldn't want to be treated the same as my first. Looking back now, I realize rather than trying to recreate what I had, I should have celebrated the uniqueness of our three.

I tried to find answers to my own questions about raising multiples in the literature. Even though a book on multiples might have said "Twins, Triplets, and More," it usually meant more twins and less triplets. Feeling isolated and frustrated in the climate of raising three babies at once, I longed to connect with other parents of multiples to see if they had similar experiences. Swimming in uncharted parenting waters, I decided to create a traveling journal. I did what every SAHM (stay at home mom) does in the eleventh hour – I created a blog site on the internet. I sat at my desk and typed away a little at a time. On our web site I posted funny events that unfolded during our week. This began when our babies were one and finished when they were five.

Parents of multiples emailed me sharing their similar stories and made comments about our web site. I found comfort in hearing other family's stories. I received more than three hundred responses to our surveys and interviewed about one hundred parents. These parents' wrote stories filled out questionnaires or talked with me personally. I talked with them while their children napped or after their kids had been put to bed. Sometimes we spoke on our cell phones while our kids played at the park. I collaborated with my new-found "Captains at sea" from neighboring ships in the safe harbor of our phones or on an "I-chat" on our computers. They were gracious about sharing their experiences from their log books and memory banks. I found parents who were on similar journeys, others further ahead in their travels guiding my footage, and some not quite as far along on their trip, interested in my recommendations. I had to find a way to share them with everyone. I tried to gather a little information from both the surveys and the interviews.

I hope that these stories do for you what they have done for me – inspired transformation and transportation. I have become a more watchful and understanding parent. I've tried to take the advice of my peers – trust more, worry less, and take more pictures. The challenges we all face as parents of multiples are not unbearable, especially if we support each other. I've been privileged to have so many people touch my life by sharing their stories with me. I have tried to represent them as accurately as possible. The open-ness with which they have been given has permitted me much leeway.

The book focuses on parenting multiples during the first five years. Each chapter is organized chronologically into, naturally, three parts. The chapter opens with a story from a parent of multiples on the chapter topic. In the first section I describe our reactions to the chapter topic. In some cases, I provide lists from a conglomeration of current trends and other professionals' guidelines. I don't pretend to be an expert in any of these areas; I only present experiences of my own and others who have been so kind as to share them with me. Feel free to add and revise more as your ship needs to steer in one direction or another.

The middle section is an interview or interviews with an expert in the field of focus. Many were famous people I knew professionally or personally. Some were recommended to me by other parents of multiples. I was fortunate to have so many very talented individuals share with me and provide their wealth of information. Interspersed through every chapter are comments from other parents of multiples who were either interviewed or who had filled out a survey. These are cherished words that have been invaluable to me along this voyage. Some of them I wrote down on post-it notes and kept on my mirror in the morning to remind me why I'm getting out of bed again.

The last section is an analysis of the answers to our surveys. The questions are ones I couldn't get answered elsewhere such as, "How much help am I going to need and for how long?" Some answers were predictable, some split down the middle, and some were surprising. Half of the parents separated their kids in school for example and more than half of them breastfed all three kids. Some answers varied according to location.

What our family has experienced by adding three is an entirely new experience. We enjoyed it so much we tried again and are thrilled to have one last child. Yes, and baby makes seven. Another lucky number we hope. Although my parents did not have triplets, it is certain that all the clichés my parents told me were true. Yes, there are "Safety in numbers," and "When you have more than one child, your love is multiplied and not divided." Having multiples or knowing someone who has them is a treasured experience appreciated best through apprenticeship. Our hands may be full, but our hearts are overflowing. Enjoy the journey, may the waters be calm when your nerves are not and may the wind blow as hard as it needs to in order to encourage you to steer as straight as you can while your team shows you the way. If the weather gets too foul remember there are more vessels that look like yours out on the horizon and light houses to help ease your journey. All you need to do is pick up a phone or shoot off an e-mail and the sun will shine again.

· · ·

CHAPTER TWO

. . . . .

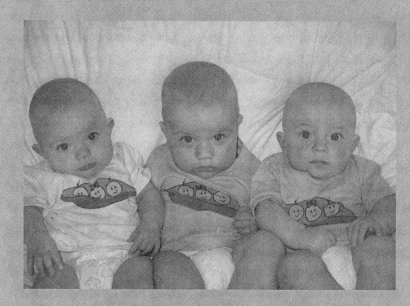

Who Has a Multiple
Pregnancy?
Or
Comrades at Sea

Beth's Story

Beth is a doctor of Chiropractic medicine who lives in Florida. Beth and her husband tried for several years to conceive. After three IUI's (Intrauterine-Inseminations) and three rounds of IVF (In Vitro Fertilization), they ended up with seven miscarriages in all. Beth decided to give up trying to have children of her own. She told me: "I was just devastated. I couldn't even function. I couldn't carry a baby to term at all."

Beth and her husband had 12 frozen embryos left, but they felt it was futile to keep trying when the embryos all ended up in miscarriages. They opted for adoption and before long had a beautiful, little, baby boy.

Beth's sister, Julie, just couldn't sit by and watch Beth go through this difficult time alone. Younger by fifteen months, she had three kids of her own and had no trouble carrying any of her pregnancies to term. She immediately found Beth a surrogate right around the time Beth and her husband had decided to adopt. But, Beth told her sister, "Thank you but we are about to adopt." The timing just wasn't' right.

When their son was a year old, Julie came to her again. "I'll surro-gate for you," she said. Beth couldn't turn her down. After all, she had 12 frozen embryos left over from all the IVF cycles. What else were they going to do with those embryos? After the thaw, only three remained.

"The doctor said, put all three in, there's no way you'll get 'em all." To everyone's surprise, all three took, "That's how I got triplets," Beth told me. There is nothing like family support. Now Julie would need Beth to help her through the pregnancy.

Beth said, "My sister was excited about the triplet pregnancy. She was ready for it and she was happy to do it. She really wanted to do it." Knowing how difficult those last couple of months can be, I asked Beth, "How did your sister manage?" Beth said, "I moved to Atlanta, (where her sister lived) for the pregnancy. I was there at every doctor's visit with her. She got put on bed rest at 27 weeks, and I took care of her and her whole family. I was like the full-time mom for six kids. It was crazy."

With all of the love and support only a sister can give, Beth helped her sister make it to 35 weeks. None of the babies had to go into NICU (Neo Natal Intensive Care Unit), not even for a day. They were happy, healthy GGB (Girl, Girl, Boy) triplets weighing in at 5.4, 5.6 and 5.9 pounds.

At the end of the interview I asked her what she thought of the comments made by the head of the ethics committee for the American College of Obstetrics who recently went on record in an article in the LA Times: "Triplets are a failed IVF. In ART (assisted reproductive technology) we are hoping for a singleton pregnancy ideally."

Beth replied, "To me, I consider a failed IVF cycle one where I didn't have a baby. I am so blessed. I have four of them. I consider them the best thing that ever happened to me. It's been really good for me. It's a lot of work, but it's like a season of life. You know what I mean? They're going to be gone and you're going to be like, where did that go? So sit back and enjoy it. Who cares if your house is a mess or it's very loud, because it's always going to be loud. You just kind of roll with it."

· · ·

Our Surveys Said...

We collected about two-hundred-and-fifty surveys from our web-based data poll. In order to participate the parents had to have access to the internet. Some had heard about our study from the "Triplet Connection" web site where it was advertised and some "hit" our web site by surfing the net looking for key words such as triplet support groups. We collected data from the time our babies were about one-year-olds to the time they were five, from 2004-2009. All of the participants who filled out a survey were asked if they would like to be interviewed. If they said "Yes" then an interview e-mail was sent to us. Putting this information together was intended to help provide some baseline by which to measure the typical day, or week, or year, in the life of a parent with multiples. Most of the parents who filled out surveys had triplets with one parent with two sets of twins and another with quadruplets.

By giving averages I don't mean to "standardize" any part of this unique adventure. If one parent chooses to nurse that should not reflect badly on someone else who chooses not to. I only present the information because I experienced opinions from others who had "expectations" for example that someone who had multiples surely wouldn't breastfeed because, let's face it, she only had two breasts, right?

I caution anyone not to use this information in a non-supportive fashion. In other words, if say the average amount of hired help parents of multiples receive is only for three months, don't assume that it is because that is all the help that is needed. Many factors were not included that would round out the figures such as whether or not parents work part time or full time and what their socioeconomic status is. Someone whose husband is home everyday at four o'clock for example versus someone whose husband works eighty hours a week may need less outside help. Likewise, someone whose mom lives next door and comes over every day may need less help.

This book is for all of you who contributed and for your families. It is difficult to understand what it is like to have more than one baby at a time unless you have walked in the shoes of a parent of multiples. Try these shoes on. They are like the 'Ruby slippers' with magical powers. With them you can visit any of our lives and feel at home. After all, "There is no place like home."

DEMOGRAPHICS

1. Location of participants in our surveys

The locations of the participants of the surveys and interviews reviewed were primarily domestic with some foreign respondents. The percentage of responses from foreign countries made up about seven percent of the amount of received. The remaining domestic responses were divided into five regions: Midwest, Northeast, Southeast, Southwest, and West. The greatest percentage of responses came from the Midwest at about twenty-six percent (see chart below). About ten percent chose not to disclose their location.

2. Ages of parents and their children from our surveys

The parents' were, on average, thirty-six years of age for the moms, and thirty-eight years for the dads. Many more moms reported their ages than did dads. The multiples on average were age four at the time the parents filled out the surveys. This is why over half of the parents couldn't comment on whether or not they had separated their kids in school, because their children weren't old enough yet to go to school. The reason this may have been a factor is because on our website we had pictures of our family and our kids between the ages of one and five over the five year span of collecting information. People may have responded who could relate to us because their children were the same ages.

3. How many girls, boys or mixed?

Through-out the book a coding of what the "gender composition" of the families triplets will appear. If they had three boys, it will say "BBB," if two girls and a boy, "GGB." If the children were identical it is stated. The distribution of possible combinations of triplets was fairly even, with more girl/boy mixed sets then all girl or boy sets. Out of 251 surveys on file, 249 were triplets. The total number of girls and boys were about the same. The groups were BBG (34.1%), GGB (31.3%), GGG (19.7%), and then BBB (14.9%).

4. Mother's occupations

Job categories were broken down into fifteen categories (see box). Since almost all of the surveys were filled out by women, the occupations were assumed to be that of the moms and not the dads. The category SAHM refers to "Stay-at-home mothers." Some SAHMs had full-time jobs before becoming full-time SAHMs. In those cases, they were sorted in the job class they used to carry. But if they had always been a full-time SAHM they were put in the SAHM category. A few entries didn't fit into the groups such as "self-employed" or "stylist." Out of 238 classified entries, the most common job categories were Business/Entrepreneurs (23.5%), stay-at-home mothers (20.2%), educators (16%), and nurses

(9.2%). These four categories made up 70% of all surveyed mothers of triplets.

5. Educational Background of the Mothers of Multiples

Education background was sorted into five possibilities: (a) high school diploma; (b) some college, (in) college, over 60 hours in college; (c) 2-year degree: AA, 2-year, 3-year degree, college graduate, or associates degree; (d) 4-year degree: BS, BA, BSM, BSN, BSW, BBA, Registired Nurse, university, 4-year, pending master's; and (e) Post-graduate/ Professional: MS, MA, PhD, MBA, Nurse Practitioner, MD, JD, post-graduate, Law Degree. Based on 237 valid surveys the greatest frequency in the education category was a 4-year degree (39.7%). The next most frequent answer for education was Post-gradate/Professional (25.3%). This means two-thirds of the participants in the survey had a four-year college degree or better.

How did you do it?

Most couples simply want to be parents and so need a way to get pregnant. None of us set out to have triplets or quadruplets. We went to fertility clinics when all else had failed. After five years of listening to peoples stories, I realized I myself was insensitive to ask this question on the survey. What was I thinking? I guess I was curious. Inquisitive people have a theory such as "Yeah, everyone I know who did IVF (in vitro fertilization) ends up with multiples."

Reflecting on my experience, the surveys, and the discussions with other parents, I realize that the true purpose of why people use assistance to get pregnant is because they want a baby. As my good friend Sandra says, "They want what 16 year olds all over this country manage to do without trying. They want a family and want to be a parent so bad that they endure the rigors of taking drugs, being pricked and prodded, and being subjected to physical pain. They want a baby so bad they do all of this for the chance it might work. They certainly do not do go through this with the aim of having multiples."

The first question that delved into the "How did you do it" scenario was "Did you have trouble getting pregnant?" Since about three-quarters of the parents sought-out assistance for fertility, it makes sense that the population sample would be, on average, a group older than thirty-five. Laura Urlick, a doula and an acupuncture specialist in the area of fertility from LA Herbs and Acupuncture put it well; "Many of the mothers who have been unsuccessful in reproduction are older and their reproductive cycle is winding down. Age is such a big factor that I think women in our society realize. It ends up being a really heart-breaking factor for so many people. It's just pushing a rock uphill sometimes because so many women, seeking acupuncture for fertility, are over 35 or 38."

It is true many triplet parents sought the help of fertility treatments to get the outcome of a multiple pregnancy. The use of fertility drugs was most common (76.7%) followed by IVF (in vitro fertilization) (47.5%), then IUI (intrauterine inseminations) (45.7%). Even though the odds are one in about nine thousand for spontaneous triplets without any intervention, I interviewed at least a half a dozen parents whose triplets were "natural." (7) According to Nancy Bowers, author of <u>The Multiple Pregnancy Sourcebook</u>, about thirty-seven percent of births from ART (assisted reproductive technology) are multiples [meaning twins or triplets]. Twin pregnancies are most common, but higher-order multiples occur about six to seven percent of the time, especially if large numbers of embryos are transferred."(10) The book was published in 2001, so the percentages may differ slightly now.

Factors that impact the results depend on the age of the mother, the number of embryos transferred, and the quality of the embryos transferred, to name a few. In our case, at age thirty-eight, if I transferred three embryos that had divided into eight cell embryos on day three, the likelihood of a triplet pregnancy was 0.4 percent (four out of one thousand). But, when we tried to get pregnant again at age forty-three, the likelihood was much less. All circumstances the same, we had a 0.003 percent (three out of one-hundred thousand) of getting pregnant with triplets. I didn't mean to be like everyone else and ask the nosy questions, but from a reporter's viewpoint, I thought some of us might want to know whether one method was more prevalent than another.

Percent of parents who used assisted fertility or had trouble getting pregnant

"I got pregnant with triplets while I was on the pill."
Alicia C., San Diego, California

6a. Percent of parents of multiples who had trouble getting pregnant

Seventy-eight percent of the parents surveyed said they had trouble getting pregnant. Keep in mind this is not the same question as did you need help or assistance getting pregnant. Some answered, "No," they didn't have trouble getting pregnant, but they did use assistance such as IVF or IUI to get pregnant. The converse was also true. Some said, "Yes," they had trouble getting pregnant, but they didn't use assistance such as fertility drugs to do so. I remember that, in talking with some of the moms who got pregnant on their own, I sensed their particular annoyance to the question "How did you do it?"

The statistics for getting pregnant with triplets without fertility drugs or "assistance" is 1/8,100-1/9,800. (7) Our survey didn't specifically ask how each parent of multiples got pregnant, but it asked if they used these means of assisted reproduction: (1) fertility drugs; (2) IUI (intrauterine inseminations; or (3) IVF (in vitro fertilization). These are the most common assisted fertility techniques. There were a few who used surrogates, but this sub-population was not separated out because in order to use a surrogate, IVF is also performed. There may be other methods of assistance I'm not familiar with, but on the survey, I focused on those methods only.

6b. Percentage of Parents of Multiples Who Tried Fertility Drugs

The next question was "Did you use fertility drugs?" Out of 240 valid answers, 184 or 76.7 percent answered "Yes" they did use fertility drugs. Keep in mind, in order to produce the eggs for harvesting (for an IVF cycle), many women may need a drug to stimulate the ovaries or improve the lining of the uterus (for an IUI cycle), so these answers may overlap; someone who took fertility drugs probably also tried IUI's or IVF.

6c. Percentage of Parents of Multiples Who Tried
Inter-Uterine Inseminations

To the question "Did you try IUIs?" Among the 230 respondents, 185 or 45.7 percent said "Yes" they tried IUI. IUI uses a catheter to place sperm directly into the uterus. The goal with IUI is to increase the number of sperm that reach the fallopian tubes and subsequently increase the change of fertilization.(8) When this method of assisted reproduction is used frequently the ovaries have been stimulated and may produce more than one egg. Depending on the age of the mother and other factors, some fertility clinics may recommend trying one to three rounds of IUIs first and if they are not successful then try an IVF procedure. The IUI procedure is less invasive and more inexpensive than the IVF procedure.

"We only put in two embryos. One split. That's how we got identicals."
Kim D., Charleroi, Pennsylvania

6d. Percentage of Parents of Multiples Who Tried In-Vitro
Fertilization

The next question was "Did you try IVFs?" Out of 247 respondents, 114 or 47.5 percent said "Yes" they tried IVF. Some of the women who tried IUIs also tried IVF, while some of them tried IVF without trying IUIs. With IVF, fertilization occurs in the laboratory, and then the embryos are placed in the woman's fallopian tube or uterus. IVF allows more control than an IUI. Couples make decisions about the number of eggs to fertilize and the number of embryos to transfer. (9)

The remaining 18.2% said they did not use fertility drugs, or have any of the two assisted reproductive technology (ART) procedures listed on the survey. Chances are they got pregnant on their own. Thirty percent of all triplets are conceived "naturally." (7)

"British Law of the Human Fertilization Board Protocol on national health services allows patients a certain number of tries and a limited number of embryos. For IVF, it used to be two embryos transferred on a fresh cycle and three embryos transferred for a frozen cycle.

We tried for five years before I had the triplets – two rounds of IUIs, four IVFs. I do feel like my three are a miracle. Even when times are hard, I can't believe they are mine. It's quite unbelievable what science can do."
Dionne C., Cardiff, South Whales, BBG

STATISTICS

1. Location
Collected from 252 questionnaires, there were 24 who either did not provide location data or were not willing to have it used in the study, while 9 other answers were potentially ambiguous. Among the remaining 219 valid answers, 6.8% of the respondents are foreign, 26% from Midwest, 21.9% from Northeast, 9.6% from Southwest, and 14.6% from the West.

2a. Parent's Age – Mothers – at time questionnaire was completed
There were 224 valid responses for mothers' age and 168 for fathers'. The mothers' ages range from 21 to 57 with an average age of 36.29 and standard deviation of 6.05.

2b. Parent's Age – Fathers – at time questionnaire was completed
The father's ages range from 24 to 64 with an average age of 38.43

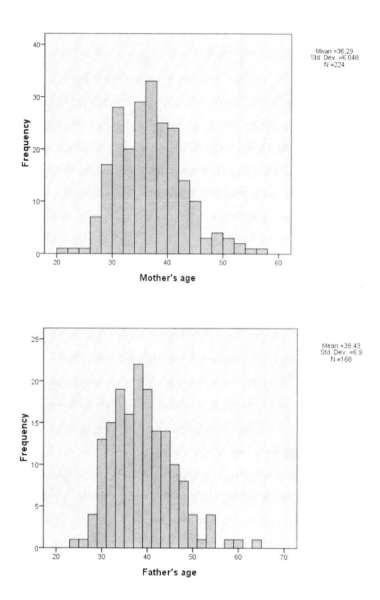

and standard deviation of 6.9. The median ages for mothers and fathers are 36 and 38, respectively while the modes are the same for two distributions.

2c. Ages of multiples at time questionnaire was completed

The range of born triplets' ages is from 6 days up to 33 years, while a handful is still waiting to be brought to this world. The average age of triplets is 4.21 years, with a standard deviation of 5.09 years. These statistics are computed from 216 valid responses. The first quartile, median, and the third quartile are found to be 1 year, 2.5 years and 5 years, respectively. This means for instance that at least 25% of the triplets in this survey are less than one year old, while about a quarter of them is old enough for grade school. The histogram of the age distribution below shows that ages are heavily right-skewed.

Age distribution of the triplets in this survey

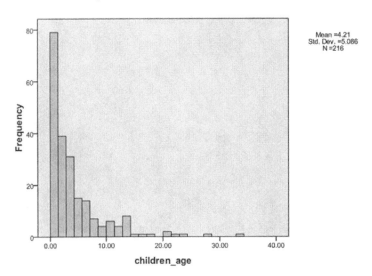

3. How Many Boys and How Many Girls?

Out of 251 triplets on file, one of them is recorded as a quadruplet (BBBG), and another one is recorded as unborn. For the remaining 249 bona-fide triplets born to this world, the percentages of "BBB", "BBG", "BGG", and "GGG" are 14.9%, 34.1%, 31.3%, and 19.7%, respectively.

The chart illustrating this composition is shown below. These numbers suggest that the total numbers of boys and girls in this survey are about the same.

Triplet Combo

	Frequency	Percent	Valid Percent	Cumulative Percent
BBB	37	14.9	14.9	14.9
BBG	85	34.1	34.1	49.0
BGG	78	31.3	31.3	80.3
GGG	49	19.7	19.7	100.0
Total	249	100.0	100.0	

4. Mother's occupations

Based on the 238 classified entries, the most common job categories are Business/Entrepreneurs (23.5%), stay-at-home mothers (20.2%), educator (16%) and nurses (9.2%). They comprise about 70% of all surveyed triplet mothers.

Occupation

	Frequency	Percent	Valid Percent	Cumulative Percent Valid
Building/Construction	1	.4	.4	.4
Business/ Entrepreneur	56	23.5	23.5	23.9
Doctor	4	1.7	1.7	25.6
Educator	38	16.0	16.0	41.6
Fitness	5	2.1	2.1	43.7
Food Service	3	1.3	1.3	45.0
Insurance	2	.8	.8	45.8
IT/Computer Sciences	10	4.2	4.2	50.0
Law	14	5.9	5.9	55.9
Medical Assistant	14	5.9	5.9	61.8
Nurse	22	9.2	9.2	71.0
SAHM	48	20.2	20.2	91.2
Student	2	.8	.8	92.0
Therapist	18	7.6	7.6	99.6
Travel	1	.4	.4	100.0
Total	238	100.0	100.0	

5. Educational Background of the mothers of multiples

	Frequency	Percent	Valid Percent	Cumulative Percent Valid
2-year Degree	30	12.7	12.7	12.7
4-year Degree	94	39.7	39.7	52.3
High School Diploma	17	7.2	7.2	59.5
Post-graduate/Professional	60	25.3	25.3	84.8
Some College	36	15.2	15.2	100.0
Total	237	100.0	100.0	

As seen in the above table, the proportions triplet moms whose achieved highest level of education being "high school", "some college", "2-year degree", "4-year degree", and "post-graduate/professional" are 7.2%, 15.2%, 12.7%, 39.7%, and 25.3%, based on 237 valid responses out of 251 survey participants.

6a. Percentage of Parents of Multiples Who Had Trouble Getting Pregnant

Out of 245 respondents who provided a valid answer, 192 or 78.4% of them answered "Yes" while 53 or 21.6% answered "No".

6b. Percentage of Parents of Multiples Who Tried Fertility Drugs

Among 240 valid answers, 184 or 76.7% answered "yes" and 56 or 23.3% answered "no."

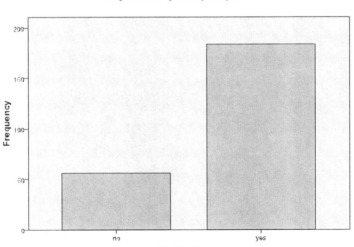

Did you use any fertility drugs?

6c. Percentage of Parents of Multiples Who Tried Intrauterine
    Inseminations

Among 230 valid answers, 105 or 45.7% of them were "yes" and 125 or 54.3% of them were "no."

6d. Percentage of Parents of Multiples Who Tried In-Vitro
    Fertilization

Out of 240 valid responses, 114 or 47.5% answered "yes" while 126 or 52.5% answered "no".

Would You Do Anything Differently?

"There is nothing I would do differently. If you always dwell on what you did wrong, you will never see the good in what you did right. You make mistakes for a reason to learn from them. When you do something wrong, do it differently the next time and just focus on the good things. That is what is important."
Elizabeth L., Wellston, Ohio
GGG

One survey in a fill in the blank question/answer portion we asked, "Anything you would do differently, or, any regrets?" I wasn't searching for anything in particular, merely inquisitive. In the chapters ahead more discussion on these topics will follow. Here are the six most frequent answers, in order of popularity:

Anything you would do differently?
- Nothing
- Asked for Help
- Established better sleep habits
- Focus more or less on the "feedings"
- Worry less
- Kept better records

1. We Would Do Nothing Differently

The overwhelming response to the question, "What would you do differently?" was "Nothing." Thirty-one percent said that, "We wouldn't change a thing." Perhaps I am a "Glass-half-empty" person because all through my internet blog columns, I went on about how I wish I had done this or that differently. Most parents did not feel the same way. Tracy R. from Edwards Air Force Base in California, summed it up: "There was never a moment we wished that anything would have turned out even slightly different."

"If I could go back, I would have done more reading on how hard it is to care for preemies. I was never exposed to one before…it is truly another ballgame. Also, I would have tried to get permission to tour a NICU. I am now in a little group and it would have been nice to meet them while I was pregnant since they really do have good advice, especially the moms with other kids and triplets."
Mary S., White Haven, Pennsylvania, BBG

2. Asked for Help

Another frequent response to the question "Anything you would do differently?" was: "We wished we would have had more help when the children were little." Some said they wish they would have accepted more of the help they were offered. Others said they would have *asked* for more help. However, it is difficult to know how to delegate work to willing volunteers. No one enjoys having more bodies around watching their parenting and activities of daily living. It is no doubt a dilemma. Deb A. from Lancer, Saskatchewan, Canada, wished she had "Hired help for the night feedings." Some privacy has to be compromised in accepting family or friends into ones' home on a regular basis; and remember, most people love babies, especially grandmas, and they can hardly wait to get their hands on those little people. Help does not only mean people in your house watching the children. They could make some meals for you, pick up groceries or even water your garden. Parents of multiples might also want to get help from other support groups. Lynda C. from Nesconset, New York, advised "Get kids in multiple groups."

3. Established better sleep habits

Many parents wished they had established better sleep habits from the onset. For some the desire was that they had kept them together in their cribs or in the same room longer. Sarah H. from Adelaide wished she had "Kept them in a cot longer." Sleep aides such as rocking them to sleep or offering a pacifier were also common regrets. "We wish we hadn't put them down with a 'binkie!' or, "We wish we hadn't give them a bottle at bedtime." Eventually, children figure out their own methods of soothing or putting themselves to sleep. None of them will go to college with a "binkie" in their mouth.

"I wish I was not influenced by the well-meaning advice of singleton moms whose experiences were vastly different than mine. I wish I would have listened to my instincts more about what my babies needed, collectively and individually." Danielle M., Acworth, Georgia

4. Focus More or Less on the "Feedings"/Breastfeeding

Several parents said that the feedings were stressful because "We would not know how much to feed or why they were crying at times." Others wished they hadn't measured the formula 'fanatically down to the drop.' It's easy to imagine that a parent would develop a preoccupation with making sure that their premature baby gets enough to eat. This concern is multiplied when all three are premature. Weight gain is one determining factor for discharge from the NICU. It makes sense parents might still worry about whether the babies are getting enough to eat when the babies come home from the hospital. One mom shared that her doctor recommended they wait to feed the babies solids until age one. She followed the advice but if she had it to do again; she would have fed her triplets solids much earlier.

Some moms wished they had nursed longer, while others wished they worried less about nursing and slept more. It was four times more common to have a mom comment that she desired to breastfed more than a mom to say she regretted breastfeeding. Some felt less connected to their children due to less nursing time. Shelley W. from Albuquerque, New Mexico, agreed: "I wish I would have breastfed longer."

"Funniest thing that happens is when people come up and ask who is older? I don't seem to quite understand that question. It's whoever the doc decided to grab out of my belly first!"
Jodi D., Akron, Ohio, BBB Triplets

5. Worry Less

Many parents said "If we had it to do over again we would worry less and trust the process more." When the babies were little, plenty of moms were worried about illnesses such as RSV (respiratory syncytial virus). Some felt guilty when all three babies would cry at once. Other felt help-less about not being able to meet the demands of all three at once. A few said that their fears early on in the pregnancy reduced their enjoyment of the birthing experience. Kelly Ann E. from Lansdale, Pennsylvania said she was "When I was pregnant with the triplets I was so worried about delivering them safely and alive that I did not really give much thought to their actual birth. As a result, I had been on magnesium sulfate; there were 30 doctors and nurses in the room. It was complete chaos. I basically missed the entire event. I would give ANYTHING to go back in time and buy a video camera and get back memories of the night that I missed. It is the most significant night of my life and I don't remember most of it. It is by far the biggest regret of my life." Murray Roberts, an old friend of the family, used to always say "Ninety percent of your worries never really happen." Not a bad mantra to follow. It is much easier "Said than done."

6. Kept better records.

Parents of multiples have to stay on top of clutter or be as organized as possible in order to survive. Photos need to be sorted, homework papers prepared, doctor's records stored, not to mention daily organization of sports equipment and laundry sorted. Some parents wished they had taken more pictures, or caught more funny moments in the babies' journals. Michaele H. said she wished she'd "Written down the funny things the kids said and did." One mom recommended taping the children's voices with a tape recorder to catch those precious sounds of youth. Even if a parent kept a journal, some were disappointed they had not kept their journals longer. Infancy goes by too fast. Personally, I enjoyed the family blog site we did on the computer. It saved time in phone calls by having a central location to report what was going on with the babies. The site also served as a storage area for pictures and journal comments so that when it came time to go to my monthly scrap book party I was prepared.

It is important to look forward as much as possible. Take heart in knowing that other parents struggled with this and can laugh now at what seemed unbearable at the time. One of my favorite stories of childhood is when my brothers secretly audio-taped my mom screaming at them. She came back in the room while they were playing back her "mini tantrum," sat down on the floor and laughed right along with them. All parents need to have a sense of humor, having more simply means more laughs to share and record.

In summary the surveys come from 250 parents who ranged in age from 36 to 38 years old. All but two were parents of triplets. The average triplets' ages were four years old. The children were equally represented with the most frequent make up being BBG triplets. All but two questionnaires were filled out by moms. The moms were from all walks of life with the largest percent in administration/entrepreneurial positions or stay-at-home mothers. More than two-thirds had a four-year college degree or better. Most were from the United States, but about 7% were foreign. Three quarters of the parents had trouble getting pregnant used fertility drugs. Some went on to try intrauterine inseminations or In-vitro fertilizations, but about 18 % got pregnant without the assistance of fertility drugs or assisted reproductive technology.

The following pages will go into more detail about what to expect when you are expecting the exceptional pregnancy. It is not intended to replace any other professional advice, merely suggestions and observations from either other professionals or professional parents of multiples. I'm not a reality television show celebrity. My work room is located in our play room, nestled in the back corner underneath a stack of bills and photos to file. I started jotting down notes to myself, tried to answer my own questions. Am I a more conscientious parent because I because I have triplets or am I an overwhelmed, frazzled parent? The answer is neither. I'm not better or worse than any other parent, but it is a unique parenting challenge that most parents at first (including myself) have difficulty "wrapping their brains around" the concept of raising three at once.

The advice I've collected in the surveys and interviews from other parents of multiples is the medication prescription I needed to get through these first five years. I hope to convey these amazing stories in the following pages. Some of the names and locations maybe altered to protect those who requested it. The stories come from my interpretation of what was discussed in our interviews or in written correspondence from parents who read my web-blogs. I wish I could have published each and every one of them. The hardest part was picking which stories on which topic knowing I would not have room for all of them. I am grateful to all those who contributed.

. . .

Bibliography
1. Dream Dinners.com
2. Ely, Leanne. <u>Saving Dinner</u>. New York, New York, 2003.
3. G. Seuss. <u>Oh the Places You'll Go</u>. New York, New York, 1990

Personal Interviews
Beth Williams
Laura Urlick, LA Herbs & Acupuncture

Resources
The American Fertility Association http://www.theafa.org

CHAPTER THREE

· · · · ·

Pregnancy – What to Expect When
You Get the Unexpected
Or
Smooth Sailing

Shelley's Story

Shelley and Herman from Albuquerque, New Mexico, were good candidates for "assisted reproductive technology." Shelley said: "We tried several different things because I couldn't conceive." Shelley was forty-two years old when they looked for assistance getting pregnant. She and her husband were lucky. Many couples who struggle with fertility issues explore assistive reproduction but are not fortunate on their first try. It's a numbers game. The more times or procedures attempted to better ones' chance of conception.

Shelley was pregnant after just one round of in vitro fertilization. She explained, "We just did one. The first one took. They implanted five [embryos]. On December 25th I did our first pregnancy test and it was positive." They not only beat the odds, but they hit the jackpot. Shelley was surprised to find out that she had more than one fetus "take." She explained: Then, on December 30th, New Year's Eve, they did the sonogram and [we saw] four – I was pregnant with quads." So, out of five implanted, four fetuses "took." Maybe Shelley's doctors should have been more cautious. After all, her sister had twins just a couple years older, and she had had two previous successful pregnancies (who by this time were teenagers).

On Shelley's survey she didn't check the box on the question "Did anyone ask you to reduce?" But in talking to me she remembered, "When we found that out I was pregnant with the quads, the doctor that we went to said he would prefer to use a selective reduction. But to me, you don't do that. To me they're living beings from God. We had real strong issues about that. So we decided we weren't going to do that."

The pregnancy was more delicate than Shelley and her husband had anticipated. She miscarried one of the fetuses at nineteen weeks and was immediately hospitalized for about four-and-a-half weeks. "I miscarried one and they told me that we would not carry all of them. That we probably should plan on just miscarrying them all. That's why they left me in the hospital, because they said I mine as well prepare myself for actually miscarrying all of them."

At almost twenty-six weeks Shelley was admitted to the hospital again, this time for pre- term labor. Shelley's background as a scrub technician probably served her well in directing her care at the hospital. Many women who have a history of miscarriage are anxious about going against their doctor's advice.

When Shelley's doctor wanted to deliver the triplets at thirty or thirty-two weeks, she didn't agree. "The girls were a pound, pound and a half, and they wanted to induce or try to do a C-section and I'm like, No!"

She ended up switching doctors. At twenty-nine weeks she left the hospital and found a new doctor and went back into the hospital at thirty two weeks until delivery just as a precaution not due to any difficulty or pre term labor. "Really just for them to keep an eye on me. I could still walk around on the floor and go off the hospital grounds for only one or two hours at a time."

Shelley ended up carrying them thirty-six weeks and five days. "I wanted to carry as long as I could. I mean, I could understand if the placenta were tearing, or the girls were stressing out, or my body was giving out, but everything was fine. Everything was going great."

At birth the girls weighed between three- and-a-half pounds and four-and-a-half pounds. They did not require oxygen for breathing, but were on room air in the nursery. They were "growers and feeders." An average triplet pregnancy is thirty-two weeks, so it is remarkable that Shelley and her babies made it as long as they did. Although she had many hurdles to over come during her pregnancy, in the end she had three beautiful girls.

• • •

What to Expect When You Get the Unexpected

"We Tried IVF five times. The funniest thing that happened so far is having a client ask me if I planned on keeping them all?"
Deanna A., General Manager at a retirement community
Summerdale, Alabama, BBG

Once a couple finds out that they are pregnant with multiples their life as they know it shifts dramatically. Questions such as "What should we do now?" and "How will we manage this pregnancy?" are the obvious ones. Two unavoidable consequences of becoming pregnant with multiples that are not as expected are the probability of going on bed rest and the possibility of being asked to reduce. Over three-quarters of the parents I spoke with had to go on bed rest at sometime during their pregnancy and more than 65% were told, "You may want to think about reduction."

It is a frightening, emotionally charged, roller coaster ride to be pregnant with multiple babies. I never for a second thought nonchalantly about how risky it was to be potentially carrying three human lives. Every day we were successful at not losing one or all of them, we had a mini celebration. Not all parents who become pregnant with multiples are as fortunate. These stories are true accounts from other parents meant to inspire and not startle other parents who may be expecting multiples. Being prepared for every aspect of the pregnancy is only the beginning of always trying to stay a step ahead. Yes, parents of multiples are out-numbered, but they can play zone defense and plan ahead. John Wooden said, "Failure to plan is planning to fail."

While I was visiting our three-day-old infants hooked up to feeding tubes and IVs, the NICU nurse said to me, "Well, isn't this what you expected? Why are you crying?" I can honestly say, "No, I never thought for a minute that being pregnant with triplets would mean not being able to hold them for a month after they were born while they were in the NICU." Knowing I wouldn't and I couldn't reduce, I certainly would never ask anyone that question. I realize some parents need to do so because of medical reasons. But, I wouldn't feel it was any of my business to know such personal information. If someone has had to make that difficult decision compassion and not suggestions are what they need.

What are we going to do now?

I will never forget the conversation we had the moment that we found out we were having triplets. It was such a funny, surreal conversation. I was sure that we were having twins. It never crossed my mind, honestly never crossed my mind that it would be more than that. And then we're sitting there at the ultrasound and I see the doctor say "Yep, there's the heart beat – oh yeah, there are two heartbeats." And then I see him turn the screen a little bit and I'm like-"Wait a minute, is that a third one?" I'm thinking, "No, maybe I'm just seeing it from a different angle." And then he turns it back and I see the other two again and the doctor and I looked at each other at the exact same time, because we both saw it at the exact same time. Then he goes: "We did talk about the risk of multiples, right?" I'm like, "Oh my God, how many are there?" And the doctor said, "So, do you guys have a minivan?" And I said "No, we have a two-seater convertible!"

Renee G., Burlingame, California
BBG

The flood of questions that pop into one's head when they first find out they are pregnant with multiples range from "Will I ever be able to see my toes again?" to "What kind of car will I need to have?" to "Is it really possible?" Perhaps, like us they may be blind-sided by another question coming from, not only outsiders, but from the very fertility people in whom they have put their trust. "Are you going to reduce?" I was approached with the "reduction" question only once during our pregnancy by our high risk Obstetrician. At the time, I didn't know what the word even meant. I thought maybe he was hinting that I needed to lose some weight. By definition "selective reduction or selective termination" is the abortion of one or more but not all embryos in a pregnancy with multiple embryos. Many parents of multiples know what this means, but it may be an unfamiliar term to a singleton parent.

How can a newly pregnant parent of multiples go about making a decision of this magnitude? Parents struggle for months to get pregnant only to triumph and turn around to find the very clinic that they worked with asking them to reconsider? The emotional and physical costs are high. Although this question may come off the tongues of medical advisers or well-meaning outsiders in a seemingly harmless fashion, the emotional turmoil for the parent of multiples is unthinkable. It seems that the insensitivity is some how never considered by people when it's not their belly full of multiples.

"My doctor said I wouldn't need to reduce, he said it's usually safe. Triplets are fine. He said, 'If you had four or five, I would talk to you about reduction. But triplets are pretty viable.'"
Erica E., San Diego, California, GGB

Why Recommend Reduction?

Reduction: A Common Question
Our online survey asks: "Did anyone ask you to reduce your triplets?" When I interviewed those who have said yes to the "reduction" question, I ask them to explain their circumstances and how they felt. More than sixty-five percent said "Yes" that someone during their pregnancy had asked them if they would consider reduction. It's a very complex issue. Liza Mundy, a columnist for the Washington Post, sums it up fairly well in her May '07 article "Too Much to Carry?": "Selective reduction is one of the most unpleasant facts of fertility medicine, which has helped hundreds of thousands of couples to have children but has

also produced a sharp rise in high-risk multiple pregnancies." (8)

Adela G. from Perrysburg, Ohio has GGG triplets. She said, "Our original doctor wanted us to reduce. He's like – 'You're all gonna die. You have to reduce. They'll be retarded or blind or dead.' I think he is completely wrong to have said that. We're at our first year and everyone's doing very well and meeting all their milestones." Another mother of triplets said that when she went to make her initial appointment with her peri-natologist, the nurse automatically said: "Oh, you're pregnant with triplets, so you're scheduling a reduction, right?" She said this "shook her to her core." Then she persisted: "No, why would you ask me that?" The nurse replied, "Oh, most women who call here pregnant with triplets are reducing." Finally, the mom said: "Well, I'm intending on keeping all three, God willing, and I'm hoping they all make it." They not only made it, but she delivered at thirty-five weeks, two to three weeks longer then than average for a triplet pregnancy. Her babies weighed between four and five pounds each. They were in the hospital only about a week.

Why some consider reduction

On reducing from five to three: "We were initially going to go down to twins – that was our recommendation from the doctor. We looked at baby C (our Michael) on the ultra-sound, he had his hand up, waving: I swear to God. And, we just had to say 'No' about the reduction, you know, we're gonna stay with three. We still have a chance. So, thank God we did." Ariana F., Wallingford, Connecticut, BBG

Being pregnant with multiples clearly puts one at risk for a variety of maternal and fetal problems including but not limited to pre-maturity, inter-uterine-growth-retardation (IUGR), pre-eclampsia and potential risks of emotional problems or learning disabilities. (7) A triplet pregnancy increases the mom's risk of developing pre-eclampsia (a sudden increase in blood pressure after the twentieth week of pregnancy) two-fold. The average triplet is born two months prematurely, significantly raising the risk of disabilities such as cerebral palsy and of lifelong damage to the infant's lungs, eyes, brain, and other organs. (8) ALB, mother of GGG triplets from Missouri, appreciated it when her high risk Obstetrician broached the subject of reduction. She said: "I know multiple moms are very sensitive on the topic and I took it more as, you know, my doctor was really interested in the best well-being for me as his patient." Her condition was unique because she had had multiple miscarriages (labeled as an "habitual aborter") and begun her triplet pregnancy initially with a set of quads. So when she lost one of the fetuses and was transferred to the high risk doctor, he told her: "I'm not upset the first quad disappeared and I certainly would be happy if baby C (referring to one of the triplets) disappeared as well."

Doctors in particular are aware of the risks. Maybe it's not so shocking after all for an obstetrician to advise about reduction. In an LA Times article ("The Abortion Debate Brought Home"), columnist Dan Neil wrote about how he and his wife were expecting quads and had to selectively reduce two for the safety of the Mom and the babies. "We said, 'Yes' we would be okay with reduction, to the fertility specialist, not really appreciating what that meant. To our delight, four (embryos) took up residence. Our initial joy, however, was tempered by the realization that we would have to lose two to keep two." The article went on to say: "I feel sorriest for our doctors. All are parents. All regard abortion with the greatest gravity." (9)

Reduction is performed by injecting Potassium Chloride into the heart of the developing fetus or fetuses. (12) Of course those of us who have successfully carried and delivered healthy triplets know that reducing any one of our viable fetuses at any time would be a heart wrenching and extraordinary painful decision. But, only through knowledge of the risks and benefits of carrying higher order multiples to term as opposed to reduction, can a family make this extremely difficult decision. Recent statistics suggest that reduction is a successful medical treatment ninety percent of the time although estimates do varry. (11)

So, for the other ten percent, the entire pregnancy is terminated or there is a risk of injury to the remaining fetuses.

In some instances, reduction might not be an option for cultural, religious, or legal reasons. One study suggests that single embryo transfer would eliminate triplets. But the data is flawed. In some countries, IVF triplets appear to have been eliminated, but the problem is masked by significant fetal reductions. (3)

Different parts of the country and different parts of the world see reduction in another light. When I asked Dionne, a Pediatric Nurse Practitioner from Bogota, Colombia, about reduction she said: "I had never heard of reducing before I joined the triplet connection and started reading some of the posts on there. Abortion is illegal here (except recently abortion in cases of rape or danger to the mother's health was approved), so it's not something that would be part of standard medical practice to discuss. And our family and friends, in general, would be against abortion, so that never came up either. The thought never crossed my mind. I don't think I even knew it was possible." She has GGG triplets, born at thirty-four weeks.

A 1994 a prospective study comparing triplet pregnancies with multi-fetal pregnancies reduced to twins showed significantly lower incidences of pre-maturity and low-birth-weight in the population that reduced. The triplet mothers that reduced also had fewer pregnancy complications. (6) In 2002, at the annual meeting of the Society for Maternal-Fetal Medicine, Dr. Richard Viscarello presented a study of non-reduced twin and triplet pregnancies versus twin pregnancies resulting from reduction which challenged this article. His poster presentation showed that patients who had a multi-fetal pregnancy reduced to twins had an increase risk for preterm labor, prolonged ante partum hospitalization, lower fetal weight and earlier initiation of continuous subcutaneous terbutaline infusion therapy compared to those with non-reduced twins. "The decision to reduce therefore should be made based on personal choice and not on expectations of improved outcomes," Dr. Viscarello said. He went on to say: "Although there is a general

consensus that multi-fetal pregnancy reduction is beneficial for gestations involving four or more fetuses, there is controversy as to whether
the procedure improves pregnancy outcome in triplet gestations." (10)

In all honesty, having experienced the high risk problems of multiples, maybe I initially would have taken the "reduction" question more
seriously. I know I wouldn't have changed my mind, but I may have done
things differently. For example, I would have definitely carried out the
bed-rest orders more dutifully. But how could others really know what
they might do, unless they had the situation presented to them? I know
I will never ask someone else to eliminate one of their children because
he or she doesn't fit in the standard family shoe box size of 2.5 kids. It
could be that the reduction question is an expression of concern about
risk, but it might also arise from a subconscious addition to the cultural
norm that Dr. Mark Evans (an obstetrician-geneticist, a pioneer in fetal
therapy) calls "the Holy Grail of the modern two-child family: one boy
and one girl – no more, no less." (8)

*Doctor's focus so much on reduction but what about all the
medical advances that have helped us go longer and have healthier
children? I think this is under reported.*

*My babies were in the well nursery the day they were born – they
stayed in the NICU for just 2 days dues to jaundice – something any
singleton could endure. Why don't we hear more about that? I was on
hospital be rest but was not on any anti-contraction medication. I had
a few contractions but did not go into labor. I had NO complications
and the babies were born during a scheduled C-section. I had no idea
that was even possible before I had mine!*

Dorinda N., Gainesville, Virginia
GGG

Bed-Rest

Think ahead: bed-rest may be unavoidable.

I'm like 'Okay, someone's cooking my meals. I can watch TV.
I can write letters to people I haven't in a long time.' But I know I had
no control over anything. It's just weird.
   Charlene H., Howell, Michigan
   BBG, Hospitalized 30 days prior to delivery

Jennie went on bed-rest for ten weeks at twenty-three weeks
gestation due to cervical incompetence. She had back pain during
pregnancy and gestational diabetes but no pre-term labor. She
delivered at thirty-four weeks, two days. The babies were in the
NICU for two-and-a-half weeks.
   Jennie H., Calfornia, GGB

I always ask two parting questions to my interviewees: "Would you do anything differently?" and "What's the greatest challenge of having triplets?" For myself, I would do one thing differently – take the bed-rest precautions more seriously. Many interviewees agreed with me. My physical therapy training made me wary of following my "bed-rest" orders to the letter as per my doctor's recommendation at twenty weeks. I also had gestational diabetes and large babies. I didn't feel any of my Braxton Hicks contractions due to my large belly. For me, prolonged bed-rest meant potential Calcium loss and the threat of "DVT" (Deep Vein Thrombosis).

I chose to not to adhere to a specific bed-rest order which included not only bathroom privileges but also walking daily and continuing all my activities of daily living.   At thirty-one weeks my water broke, so I don't recommend this method of bed-rest. For multiples, bed-rest should be taken seriously. There's no doubt that inactivity will minimize uterine contractions. If, like in my case, uterine contractions can not be easily felt, then universal modification of activity is imperative. There are exercises that can be done while on bed-rest that will minimize the negative impact of immobility.

When bed-rest is ordered, be careful of ambiguous directions. Some women interpret bed-rest to mean resting frequently and so create a different scenario than what is intended. Gail Pekalis, my expert interviewee for this chapter, and I agree that women should get their doctors to give specific guidelines. Ask such questions as: "Do you mean bed-rest with bathroom privileges only, showers once a day or every other day?" Or ask him if he has a handout to follow. Gail adds: "Most women are afraid. They have no idea what they can do. They get so frustrated or uncomfortable they'll get up and walk around or go to a movie or go for a drive in the car. In terms of exercise, they'll ask 'Can I move? Can I do this or that?' They have no confidence in what's okay, or what they can or can't do. That's why I think it's so important to have some kind of basic protocol of what is safe to do."

It is important to remember also that the bed-rest protocol may change as the pregnancy progresses or as conditions for the mother change. Mrs. J. reminded me of this when she commented, "I experienced contractions beginning at fourteen weeks and was put on light bed-rest. Then more strict bed-rest at twenty-five weeks (bathroom priviledges only). I was monitored at home by home health nurses and usually averaged about twenty contractions per hour. I was treated with Procardia (long term) and Benadryl on an as needed basis to slow contractions."

As a foremost Women's Health Physical Therapy specialist Elizabeth Noble once said; "Nobody really knows how to start or stop labor; if we did, we'd really have something!" Many practitioners believe inactivity is likely to deter per-term labor. Preterm labor is generally defined as delivery before thirty-seven weeks. In more specific terms, it is the association of uterine contractions with changes in the cervix. Symptoms may include a sense of pelvic fullness, recurrent labor contractions (eight or more per hour), vaginal discharge, bleeding, ruptured membranes (fluid loss from the vagina) or cramping. For high-order multiple gestations, preterm labor occurs ninety percent of the time. (2)

The goal in higher order multiples is to keep the babies in the womb as long as possible. Bed-rest helps accomplish this goal. "As the pregnancy progresses, the combined weight of the babies strains the cervix. Gravity increases the pressure. Alleviating the pull of gravity and the pressure on the cervix can help prolong the pregnancy. That can be accomplished by staying off your feet and lying horizontally in bed." (4) Pam K. from New Orleans, Louisiana, felt slightly regretful. She had a set of beautiful BBB identical triplets who had no major medical issues. Still, she commented if she could do it over again, "I would have taken it easier at the end of my pregnancy possibly to avoid the pre-eclampsia. I think I overdid it, and I wish I could have been pregnant longer, even though the boys were very healthy."

Think in terms of a uterus as having finite capabilities when trying to maintain a pregnancy with more than one baby. The uterus is simply a muscle, a smooth muscle. This means it is not under direct volitional control, like the bladder, for example. Because it is a smooth muscle, the uterus can not be controlled by activation like skeletal muscles. Each woman's uterus has an innate ability to contract. A woman may be able to influence her uterus indirectly by remaining calm and inactive and so as to keep it from contracting.

In the case of a multiple pregnancy, contractibility of the uterus is obviously over-taxed and the uterus can easily contract irregularly and pre-maturely. My peri-nataligist put it very bluntly to me: "The uterus is not made to carry three fetuses." Keep in mind, the greater the number of fetuses, the greater the uterine activity. Other factors can also affect uterine activity such as time of day, hormone levels, gestational age, presence of infection, any inflammation of neighboring organs (appendicitis for example) and emotional stress levels. (2)

Pre-term labor is a common problem in high-order multiple pregnancies. In our surveys pre-term labor was the most common reason for hospitalization. The next most frequent reason for hospitalization was pre-eclampsia. Pre-eclampsia is a medical condition where a sudden increase in blood pressure or pregnancy induced hypertension occurs with significant amounts of protein in the urine, usually after the 20th week of pregnancy. Shortening of the cervix was the third reason for bed-rest which occurred in a smaller amount of multiple pregnancies. The remaining reasons moms of multiples were hospitalized for bed-rest were due to non-specific reasons or to receive steroid shots. The number of women who were on bed-rest during their pregnancy was 75.5%. The average gestational age of the babies when the moms went on bed-rest was twenty-three weeks and the average length of time they went on bed rest was eight weeks.

Uterine activity is increased by physical activity and is decreased by bed-rest. Although bed rest alone has not been shown to prevent pre-term labor, every woman who has been pregnant with triplets will confirm that bed-rest decreases the frequency of contractions. Bed-rest means "Remaining horizontal." "No cleaning out the closet, no hauling out the boxes of pictures to organized, no rolling a ball on the floor with your toddler." (1)

If symptoms of preterm labor recur, bed-rest alone will not be enough and tocolytic drugs may be necessary. Two common tocolytic drugs are magnesium sulfate and terbualine. These are given intra-venously in an attempt to relax the uterine muscle. If preterm labor continues to be a threat, betamethasone (a steroid) is administered. This enhances the babies' pulmonary maturity. "It stimulates the fetal lungs to begin producing proteins for lung operation." (2)

A unique problem with preterm labor occurs when multiples in the uterus are larger than normal. Women pregnant with larger multi-ples rarely feel contractions because the uterus is already stretched so taut that they don't feel it getting any harder. Sometimes gestational diabetes occurs in multiple pregnancies and with gestational diabetes, the babies are usually larger. Janet Bleyl contacted more than three thousand mothers who had delivered larger multiples, and very few had been able to detect preterm labor. She recommends expectant moms of multiples do home monitoring. Bleyl recommends that home monitoring be done twice a day beginning at twenty weeks. (3)

EXERCISES TO DO WHILE ON BED-REST

Do these three to five times a day for three to five times each.

Abdominal isometrics – Deep breathing with abdominal wall tightening on an outward breath. Hold the muscles only as long as your breath is exhaling.

Foot Exercises – Stretch toes up and down, side to side and in circles.

Extension isometrics – Stretch out the kinks by pressing legs and arms into the bed while exhaling or breathing out.

Pelvic Floor Exercises – On an outward breath, tighten pelvic floor muscles and hold for as long as you breathe out. Also, do quick contractions, as quick as a wink ("wink your eye, wink your anus" is the cue).

Pelvic Tilts – Take a deep breath and arch your back. Breathe out tilting your pelvis back, belly button to the floor.

Leg Slides – Breath in and as you breath out, drag your heel up the bed (or along the side of the other leg if you are side lying). Bring it down and repeat with the other leg.

Arm Exercises – Move the hands, elbows, and shoulders in all directions. Start at the hands lifting fingers up and down and moving wrists side to side. Bend elbows up and down. Lift arms straight up and down with elbows straight. With every movement exhale on exertion. Make sure you don't hold your breath.

The most important aspect of doing exercises while on bed-rest is maintaining a proper conscious, breathing pattern that enforces exhalation with all exertion. "You must exhale with each movement. Exhaling will prevent increases in pressure on your abdomen and fluctuations in circulation that occur with straining. Without proper breathing you may do more harm than good (3)." "Sidelines" is a web-based support group for women on bed rest. They post articles for moms on bed-rest. Below is a clip from their magazine. Their website is: www.sidelines.com. Moms of multiples can get valuable information from sidelines and other multiples support groups (see list in chapter seven).

Some Things To Do For A Mom On Bed-Rest

- Bring her a pint of ice cream
- Do her laundry or fold clothes while you visit
- Bring her some scented lotion or shower gel
- Lend her books about childrearing
- Give her a pedicure and paint her toenails
- Change the sheets on her bed
- Fluff up her pillows
- Bring her some Chapstick and breath mints
- Call her on the phone...often
- Send her a card for no reason
- Visit her at home or in the hospital (but make it short)
- Bring her a flower from your garden (or freshen up existing gift bouquets)
- Bring her old magazines
- Buy her the latest book on the best seller list
- Take her a bottle of flavored sparkling water
- Bring her take-out food from her favorite restaurant
- Shave her legs and rub on heavy cream
- Remind her of the wonderful thing that she is doing!

Since bed-rest was so prevalent in the parents we surveyed and they were all parents of three or more, my advice is to take the idea of bed-rest more seriously than we did. Ceclia W. from Boston, Massachusetts had regrets as we did. Cecilia was hospitalized at twenty-three weeks for preterm labor and dialation. She was in the hospital for two months and then on strict bed-rest at home for a month. She said, "My original goal was thirty-seven weeks, but I gave birth at thirty-four weeks and five days. I would've tried to go longer, thirty-five or six week, with the pregnancy, but I was induced to try to deliver vaginally – all three were head down in position. In the end I had a c-section.

What I might do differently is to try modified bed-rest earlier to avoid hospital bed rest."

Try to get guidelines from your physician and talk to other parents of multiples about what they did. Getting connected early on in one's pregnancy with multiples is extremely beneficial. Kitty L. from St. Louis, Missouri was pregnant with GGB triplets. She commented, "I wish I would have made more of an effort pre-pregnancy to connect with other triplet families." It may be a time of shock when one finds out they are pregnant with multiples at first. As that shock wears off it is time to get connected. Other parents of multiples are out here and we are willing to share our stories and to help. It is a difficult time and it will be more difficult if one is isolated.

What the Expert's Say
Gail Pekalis, PT, Owner of Women's Physical Therapy in Beverly Hills and Santa Monica

Gail Pekalis is a physical therapist who specializes in "Women's Health." She's been seeing mothers of multiples on bed-rest in their homes or at their hospital rooms for over twenty years. She owns and manages "Women's Physical Therapy" in Beverly Hills and Santa Monica. She is a mother of four and a grandmother of two. Her advice comes not only from her women's health physical therapy practice, but also from her personal experiences.

I asked her, "What is the average length of time someone with multiples will be on bed-rest? And, at what gestational stage will a doctor typically put a woman who is having two or more on bed-rest?" She said; "You know, there really isn't an average, but I've seen as early as 17 weeks or as late as 35 or 34 weeks to get them to go until 36 or 37 weeks. It depends if they have had a cerclage or not and at what point they've had the cerclage." A cerclage is the placement of sutures at the introdus to prevent premature labor. It may be necessary if the walls of the vagina are thinning. Some of the moms I interviewed had this operation, but it was not a universal procedure. Bed-rest was a universal recommendation for the majority.

Bed-rest can be an order the doctor gives at a certain gestational stage in the pregnancy. For example, my doctor wanted me to be on "bed rest" and off work at twenty weeks. I was on my feet all day in a physical therapy practice. My doctor would have wanted me to go on bed-rest at twenty weeks regardless of how physically active my job was. Some women I talked to who had more sedentary jobs were able to work up until their delivery, while others went on bed rest at a certain point regardless.

Usually, if labor begins prematurely, strict bed-rest is ordered which usually means staying in bed all of the time except for bathroom privileges. If contractions can be minimized, then bed-rest at home continues; otherwise hospitalization is necessary in order to more closely monitor labor. Once hospitalized, sometimes physical therapy may be ordered to help maintain muscle integrity, as well as improve circulation, and relaxation. Gail added: "There really is a lot physiologically going on. There's so much happening with your body. That's why physical therapy is so important; because you do need to restrict yourself in certain aspects but that has implications. So, if you can do exercises that are safe and non-weight-bearing, and of course, have any kind of manual tissue work along with the exercise, it's ideal."

I asked Gail what her protocol was for seeing patients in the hospital on bed rest. She said; "When I go in, it depends on the contraindications, what they are in the hospital for. I do have a protocol. I'll do either just upper extremities and any kind of active therapeutic exercise. If everything is ok, I'll add a one pound can or weight. If they have something in their room, like a bottle of water, I'll use that. All the exercises are done in left-side-lying position and I go through from the foot all the way up. With their ankles I do manual resistance, but I give them a program that's safe to do on their own. It's just all the way from their feet up to their shoulders. If they can sit at the bedside, I'll do neck range of motion (ROM) and shoulder ROM. If they can't sit up, then I say, 'If you have bathroom privileges and when you are up going to the bathroom, then circle your shoulders or roll your neck'. "

She continued; "I'll put it in their protocol that they have to do it when they are already vertical. I always recommend getting a shower chair, and I'll say 'do your shoulders', 'do your neck when you're up already in the shower', don't get up separately to do it. I have a protocol that is just basically active assistive, some resistive ROM and I don't do any Theraband or anything like that for the lower extremities at all. Also, some doctors order the TED hose, anti-embolitic-stockings." TED hose are tight stockings worn on ones' legs to prevent blood clots. They are usually worn by moms on bed-rest in the hospital because they are confined to bed and not able to get up and move around a lot.

In the literature, some sources may refute any exercises during a period of bed-rest, for fear that activity will cause contractions. I asked Gail if by doing exercises at bedside, anybody ever went into labor. She replied; "I've never had that problem. Actually, about ten years ago, I did a study on high risk pregnancy and the effects of physical therapy. I monitored the pregnant women before the exercise program and afterwards. The results were that they were having fewer contractions because, number one they were breathing better, and, number two, they weren't in pain. After manual therapy, they felt better so they had less pain, they were breathing and there were fewer contractions. It wasn't a huge randomized, controlled hundred and fifty person study, but it was a sample and there were no problems."

I have known Gail for over twenty years and she has been doing Obstetrics Physical Therapy for at least as long as that. She has seen moms of multiples in their homes and in the hospital while they were on bed-rest. She has taught numerous courses and trained other physical therapists as well. She continues, "It's been many years. No one has complained about having more contractions."

Modifications in activity mean no aerobic activity that will raise the heart rate to a certain level determined by ones doctor. My peri-natalogist said I couldn't bring my heart rate above one-hundred-and-fifty beats per minute. I noticed even walking in the pool brought my heart rate above this level and I used to teach pre-natal water aerobics when I was pregnant with my first child with no problems in heart rate at all. Gail warns, "Obviously, [there would be problems] if someone got up and power-walked, or someone went to the gym or someone did exercises incorrectly – which is what most people do. They do exercises incorrectly by straining or holding their breath, a 'Valsalva.'" What Gail suggests is a monitored exercise program. She also recommends activities that will not unnecessarily strain the back or joints in general. She says, "So if they [moms of multiples] are supervised and they are doing non-weight-bearing exercise, it's effective. Especially if you couple that with soft tissue work and especially if you do a lot of breathing work, it's helpful."

People tend to lump all exercise into one category, going to the gym or an aerobics class. These exercises are not appropriate in different circumstances and bed-rest is certainly one of those. The dangers of these exercises are either that the movement themselves are too strenuous or that they are done incorrectly by the person straining or holding their breath. This is referred to as 'Valsalva.' Proper supervision and non-weight-bearing exercises are safe and effective.

Many concerns run through a mother's head when she has to get off her feet and take it easy because the pregnancy is at that stage. Isolation is one concern of people on bed-rest. In our "Westside Mother's of Multiples" group that meets monthly, we take a moment each meeting to pass out cards. After all of us sign the cards for our mothers on bed-rest, a group of us go to visit the Moms and deliver cards along with magazines and puzzles. Gail commented; "Yeah, many on bed-rest feel that no one understands them. It's just so good that [these] women realize that they are not alone. I don't know if [all] women realize that there are a lot of women on bed-rest; well more and more at least these days."

Another problem is that the expectations of the spouse or partner may put undue pressure on the circumstances surrounding bed-rest. As a physical therapist privy to the family dynamics, Gail shared a story that exemplifies this concern. "There are so many different stories. There's this one I remember. This couple was just recently married and they hadn't planned on getting pregnant when they found out that they were expecting twins. Prior to that, they had enjoyed line dancing and so the husband kept asking me, 'When do we get to go line dancing again?'"

Gail told the husband, "First of all, you two will be able to go line dancing again only when you're no longer on bed-rest and second of all, once you have these babies [they were pregnant with twins], they are going to be a priority which means the dancing may not be as often." She continued, "There's a feeling of tension in any marriage when a woman is on bed-rest. The spouse is really required to pick up and do a lot of extra work, especially if they don't have any kind of help, such as family or what-have-you."

Gail reminded me, "When you are on bed-rest for the first time, it's very challenging because you think, 'This is the hard part,' and it's not the hard part. In retrospect, it's not really the hard part; when you've been through it, and you've seen it, and you're on the other side, you just know you want to make it as easy as possible for other women so that they can kind of enjoy it. You want to comfort and forewarn them to rest and relax. That way they can know that, when the hard part comes, they can handle it.

· · ·

Our Surveys Said

Regarding Questions on Reduction
1. Percentage of Parents of Multiples Who Were Asked to Reduce

Out of two-hundred-and-fifty-two responses, there were two-hundred-and-twenty-seven valid answers. Sixty-four percent answered

"Yes" while thirty-six percent answered "No.". Of these responses a statistical majority of the parents of multiples were indeed asked to reduce. It might have been interesting to know what percentage actually did reduce. I did not ask this question on the questionnaire but a few moms volunteered this information in their interviews.

2. Was There a Correlation Between Location and Whether or Not Parents of Multiples Were Asked to Reduce?

The data was then recalculated to see if there was a correlation between the location and whether or not the parents had been asked to reduce. The analysis suggests that whether or not parents of multiples are asked to reduce does depend on their location. In particular, parents in the northeast, southeast and west regions were more often asked to reduce, while parents in foreign and U.S. southwest regions have shown some of the lowest proportions of being asked to reduce. It is tempting to believe that this reflects possible differences in social and political influences in these regions, rather than medical reasons for making reduction recommendations or inquisitions.

STATISTICS

Comparison among the regions for the reduction question

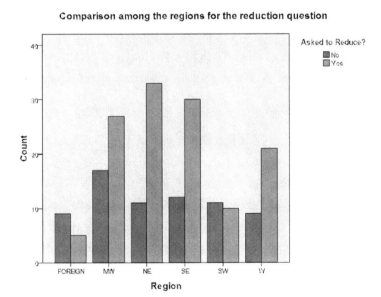

1. Percentage of Parents of Multiples Who Were Asked to Reduce

64.3% of triplet moms were asked to reduce, that is 146 out of 227. The rest 81 or 35.7% were not asked to reduce.

2. Was There a Correlation Between Location and Whether or Not Parents of Multiples Were Asked to Reduce?

Since some of the respondents were not asked the question for reduction, there are a little fewer people who did provide an answer for the reduction question as well as geographical data. For those 195 who did so, it is found that there are 35.7%, 61.4%, 75%, 71.4%, 47.6%, 70%, 64.6% of respondents who were asked to reduce from the groups – foreign, Midwest, northeast, southeast, southwest, and west, respectively (refer to the cross-tabulation table below).

Asked to Reduce Crosstabulation

region			Asked to Reduce N	Asked to Reduce Y	Total
FOREIGN	Count		9	5	14
	% within region		64.3%	35.7%	100.0%
	% within Asked to Reduce		13.0%	4.0%	7.2%
MW	Count		17	27	44
	% within region		38.6%	61.4%	100.0%
	% within Asked to Reduce		24.6%	21.4%	22.6%
NE	Count		11	33	44
	% within region		25.0%	75.0%	100.0%
	% within Asked to Reduce		15.9%	26.2%	22.6%
SE	Count		12	30	42
	% within region		28.6%	71.4%	100.0%
	% within Asked to Reduce		17.4%	23.8%	21.5%
SW	Count		11	10	21
	% within region		52.4%	47.6%	100.0%
	% within Asked to Reduce		15.9%	7.9%	10.8%
W	Count		9	21	30
	% within region		30.0%	70.0%	100.0%
	% within Asked to Reduce		13.0%	16.7%	15.4%
Total	Count		69	126	195
	% within region		35.4%	64.6%	100.0%
	% within Asked to Reduce		100.0%	100.0%	100.0%

A chi-square test was performed to check the dependency of binary answer to the reduction question on respondents' locale. The Pearson chi-square statistic is found to be .046, which is less than .05, suggesting that (with 5% level of significance) whether or not triplet moms are asked to reduce does depend on their location. In particular, northeast, southeast and west see the highest ($>= 70\%$) proportions of "Yes" to the question of reduction, while foreign and U.S. southwest have shown some of the lowest proportions.

Regarding Questions on Bed-Rest

For the prenatal section we asked several questions. I wanted to know what percentage actually went on bed-rest, for how long and whether or not that required hospitalization. I also wanted to know how far along there were when they were put on bed-rest. As earlier stated, during my pregnancy I was under the impression this would never happen to me but I was wrong. More than three quarters of the moms of multiples surveyed answered these questions and here's what we found:

- 75.5 percent had to go on bed-rest

- Ten weeks (10.27 weeks) was the average length of time on bed-rest

- The amount of time on bed rest ranged from four days to 32 weeks

- 90 percent were put on bed-rest for less than 20 weeks

- 24 weeks gestation (23.70 weeks) was the average number of weeks in gestational the mothers were when they were put on bed-rest

- The gestational age ranged between 8 and 29 week.

- 2 out of every 3 (67.20 percent) were hospitalized when put on bed-rest

- 20 days (19.80) was the average length of time hospitalized for bed-rest

- Over 50 percent were hospitalized for less than three weeks
- The amount of time hospitalized ranged from a couple hours to 182 days

STATISTICS ON BED-REST

1. Percentage of Moms Who Went on Bed-rest

There are 243 valid answers to the question of whether or not the mothers in the survey went on bed rest. It is found that 59 or 24.3% answered "no" while 184 or 75.7% answered "yes". That is, about three quarters of triplet moms went on bed rest.

Did you go on bed rest?

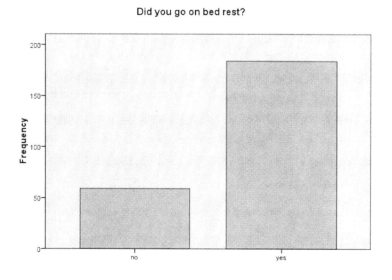

2. Amount of Time on Bed-Rest on Average

For those who went on bed rest, the length of bed rest varies from 4 days to 32 weeks. The mean and standard deviation can be found to be 10.3 and 6.4 weeks, respectively. However, the distribution of the length shows positive skewness as well as two modes, one around 6 weeks and the other around 10 weeks. The vast majority (over 90%) went to bed rest for less than 20 weeks.

How long were you on bed rest (in weeks)?

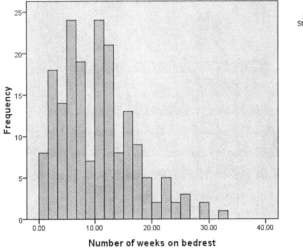

Number of weeks on bedrest

3. Gestational Age of Fetuses When Put on Bed-rest

How many weeks along were you when you were put on bed rest? The variable that counts how many weeks along those triplet moms were when they were put on bed rest shows a range between 8 and 35 weeks, with a mean of 23.38 and standard deviation of 5.77 weeks. The histogram indicates that most people had been around 20 or 25 weeks along when put on bed rest.

How many weeks along were you when you were put on bed rest?

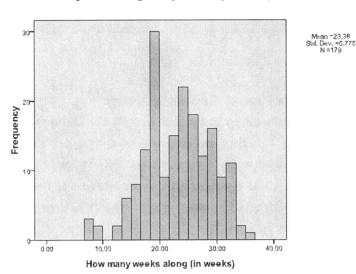

How many weeks along (in weeks)

4. Percent of Moms Hospitalized for Bed-rest

Regarding the question on hospitalization, 80 out of 244 answered "no" while 164 answered "yes". The corresponding proportions are 32.8% for "no" and 67.2% for "yes". About every 2 out of 3 were hospitalized. 7 people mentioned that they were hospitalized multiple times.

5. Amount of Time Hospitalized for Bed-rest

For those who were hospitalized, the length varies from couple of hours or overnight to as many as 102 days. The length of hospitalization in weeks has a mean of 19.80 and a standard deviation of 22.18. Over half of the people left the hospital within 3 weeks. The distribution is positively-skewed.

Length of hospitalization in days

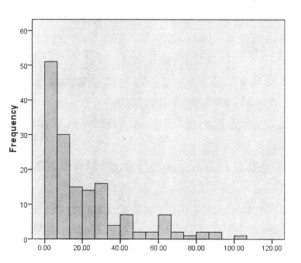

Bibliography on Reduction

1. Bowers, Nancy. Multiple Pregnancy Sourcebook. New York, New York, 2001

2. Fertilitycommunity.com

3. J Gerris. The near elimination of triplets in IVF. Reprod. Biomed. Online. Vol 15, No. 3. pp. 40-4. 2007.

4. http://www.americanpregnancy.org/infertility/iui.html

5. http://www.childbirthsolutions.com/articles/pregnancy/oddmulti/index.php

6. Liptz, Shlomo, Reichman, Brian; Uval Jefet, Shalev, Josef; Achiron, Reuven; Barkai, Gad; Lusky, Ayala; Mashiach, Shlomo. A Prospective Comparison of the Outcome of Triplet Pregnancies Managed Expectantly or by Multi-fetal Reduction to Twins. American Journal of Obstetrics & Gynecology. Vol. 170, No . pp. 874-879, March 1994.

7. AM Moore, K O'Brien. Follow-up issues with multiples. Paediatr. Child Health. Vol 11, No 5. pp 283-6, 2006.

8. L Mundy. Too Much to Carry? , May 20, 2007; W14, washington-post.com

9. D Neil. The Abortion Debate Bought Home, May 6, 2007; latime.com

10. N Walsh. Triplet Reduction to Twins Provides No Major Benefit: Smaller Babies and Earlier Deliveries Seen, March 1, 2002; OB/GYN News; findarticles.com

11. C Williams, A Sutcliff. Infant outcomes of assisted reproduction. Early Hum. Dev. Vol. 85, No. 11. pp 673-7, 2009.

12. ZFCKA Zhi. Clinical study of selective multifetal pregnancy reduction in second trimester. Vol. 42, No. 3. pp 152-6, 2007.

Bibliography on Bed-rest

1. Agnew, Connie, Klein, Alan, and Ganon, Jill . <u>Twins! Pregnancy, Birth, and the First Year of Life</u>. . New York, New York, 1997.
2. Keith, Louis, Blickstein, and Isaac. <u>Triplet Pregnancies and Their Consequences.</u> London, UK, 2002.
3. Noble, Elizabeth. <u>Having Twins.</u> Boston, Mass, 1991.
4. Fierro, Pam. <u>The Everything Twins, Triplets, and More Book.</u> Avon, Mass, 2005.

Personal Interviews
Gail Pekalis, PT
Shelley Williams

Bed Rest Organization www.sidelines.com.

CHAPTER FOUR

· · · · ·

*Breastfeeding – the Quest for Three
Breasts
Or
Navigating Nursing*

Karen's Story

Karen S. from Gilbert, Arizona had a breastfeeding goal for her GGB triplets: nurse them all for one year. "I told them when they turn one, that's it; no boobs, no bottles, here's your cup." And that is what she did.

Being newly pregnant with triplets, Karen knew her beautiful thirteen-and-a-half-month-old baby girl would still need lots of attention but, some unexpected challenges awaited her. She didn't foresee that her triplets in their first months of life would have problems with reflux or the fact that they would all go back to the hospital due to RSV.

Karen coaches a high school girl's basketball team and is a teacher. As head coach for the team how could she predict that within the year the team would not only win the league, but also go on to state finals before she delivered her triplets.

Although she was thirty-two years old when the triplets were born, her doctor allowed her to continue coaching as long as she didn't go into preterm labor. She made it the entire season, delivering at thirty-four weeks and one day.

"The only game my doctor told me I couldn't coach was the last game of the season, the state championship. I had pre-eclampsia and my kidneys would just shut down. I spent the night before the game in the hospital and the doctor said, 'Can you please skip the championship?' I was like, 'Are you kidding?,' but, I skipped it." Her husband is a data base administrator who works from home a few days a week. Luckily for her, he loves all sports and was willing to help her out in a pinch.

"My husband went and sat right behind the bench and I was calling in plays. You could see him on TV behind the bench talking on the phone."

Once she delivered, she had one of the three (Mark) stay right in the room with her. Since he didn't go to NICU, he latched on right away, meanwhile, for the other two, she pumped for the following two months. Her challenge now was not milk production but dealing with the babies not keeping the milk down.

All three were babies "refluxers" which meant they all had acid reflux in the first few months. She commented to me: "The reflux was just hard. We were both exhausted, you know? I don't know if you remember the baby days, but I remember we'd be out to dinner, just my husband and myself, and I would hear babies crying echoing in my head. Or, in the shower, I would hear babies crying because they cried a lot." It was just one extra thing to worry about.

At two months, one of the girls latched on. Now she was able to nurse two babies and pump for the third. At six months Karen went to pumping and putting the milk in cups for them. "I was adamant that they start 'sippys' at six months." She was able to do this for an entire year. Karen was an amazing example of a nursing mother extraordinaire.

She even pumped while coaching at times. One of her funniest stories was when she was nursing on the basketball bench. "There's the time I was breast-feeding on the bench. I fed the first kid, finished up, burped 'em, handed him over-my sister sits next to me. I was like, here, Karla can you take this one and I was onto the next. They would hand me another baby to start feeding. My sister turns around and he's like, what are you doing? I was feeding them. What do you think I'm doing. You know, she was just absolutely appalled. She's like, whoa, whoa, whoa. You're not feeding them on the bench. And, I'm like, they're hungry. I'm sitting here, you didn't notice. I fed them for ten minutes and you didn't even notice. So, I admit I was kinda caught up in the craze of it all-cuz I really think that nursing moms do go a little crazy. It's okay, you kinda have to be that dedicated to really make it last."

"I was just one of those lucky people and I had a lot of milk. My pumping world record was 33 ounces in one sitting."

In response to how she juggled the triplets with her older daughter...

"Watching all my kids hovered over a ladybug in the yard, seeing the world together at the same time. Seeing them discovering the world together has been such a gift. Because when you only have one, or your kids are spread apart they discover it in their own way, but it's always alone. And I think that that is one of those things that I feel is such a gift. You can't really express or put that into words, but I wish I had known. I wish I had known cuz I cried so much for my oldest. 'Oh, I felt so bad for her' I would think but look, she's got a whole houseful of playmates."

"Before the triplets, I think my viewpoint was so limited. I was worried about my oldest child. I thought what is this gonna do to her? How is her life gonna change, you know? And now my kids are six and I've seen them growing up and everything. I just wish I could find the words to express to future parents of multiples just how amazing the experience has been. How I feel like my whole mindset has shifted and opened to this possibility of the incredible journey."

· · ·

"Although things may seem impossible in the beginning, it does get better. Always tell yourself, 'This is only temporary time.'"
Jamie G., Pittsburgh, Pennsylvania, BBB Triplets
Nursed all three for four-and-a-half months

"My children were unable to successfully breastfeed due to pre-maturity and it was too draining on all of us. If they could have fed easier, I think we would have lasted longer."
Sunny H., Tennessee, BBG born at 32 weeks
Breastfed all three for eight weeks

"Something I would have done differently? I would make sure that I asked that there be a breast pump waiting in my room for me when I got there."
Stephanie K., Chicago Heights, Illinois, GGB
Nursed all three, thirteen weeks

"We had latching problems so they were never great nursers. For a couple feedings a day I would at least attempt to breastfed somebody. I was so adamant about pumping. I pumped for almost four months."
   Lucinda S., Wankegan, Illinois, GGB

Nursing Multiples: The Quest for the Third Boob

More triplets are breastfeed than given formula. Sixty-five percent of the Moms of multiples from our surveys either pumped or nursed their babies as long as they could. The majority made it for the first few months. One Mom nursed all three of her babies exclusively for eighteen months. How can this be possible? Maybe it is because the parents of multiples in our surveys were older when they conceived their children or maybe it is because more used assisted fertility techniques or maybe still it is because these parents already made a decision to commit to twins or triplets and not reduce to singletons. What ever the reason(s) are, it appears moms of multiples all want to provide the best for their little ones.

We have been inundated with medical advice through the media that breast milk is better for babies than the best formula. Studies show older women are more likely to breastfeed than younger. Women in our surveys on average were thirty-six years old. Any woman who gets pregnant after the age of thirty-five is considered "older" than average and has heard the phrase "Your biological clock is tickin' honey" more than once in her life. Given the age factor, it makes sense that more than three-quarters of these parents surveyed had trouble getting pregnant. The journey to get pregnant may have taken longer. When you think that many triplets were conceived by assisted fertility it only makes sense that this group of Moms would do anything for their children. Moms of multiples will go through any amount of inconvenience because they have thought about the possibility that this may never have happened. Finally, most parents already had to make the decision to commit to triplets and not reduce; therefore they already made that commitment to raise their babies to the best of their abilities, which means breast milk.

Personally, when I found out I was having multiple babies, nursing was definitely not my first concern. Other major dilemmas preoccupied me, such as: how many long hours will I go without anti-contraction medications? Will my belly explode? Can we afford to send them all to college at the same time? These questions were flooding my brain, not whether or not I could truly produce enough milk for three at once. It would have helped me to know that the majority of our Moms could and did produce plenty of milk.

The last thing I want to do is promote any anxiety or guilt about nursing or not. I want to present what others have shared in the spirit of sharing and caring. We all do the best we can with what we are given; none of us should be persecuted or feel badly for doing a job most people wouldn't sign up for in the first place. Breastfeeding, especially if it hurts, can often result in the mother resenting the baby, or not wanting the baby to be so close. Bonding may be hard enough to do if one's darling babies have to spend even an hour in the NICU due to prematurity. Keep this in mind and figure out what works best for you and your family.

There are no guidelines for specifically nursing twins, triplets, or higher order multiples. However, for singletons, there are standards of practice put out by the Canadian Pediatric Society, The American Academy of Pediatrics Section on Breastfeeding, and the World Health Organization which all recommend exclusive breast feeding for the first six months. (1) Interestingly, the average duration of nursing singletons in developed countries is three months, but in developing countries it is three years. (2) Maybe this says something about the inconvenience of breast feeding and maintaining a busy life style found in developing countries.

The health benefits for both the mother and child are well-documented. It boosts the immune system for the baby or babies, aids jaw, teeth and facial development, increases maternal bonding, and reduces the risk of breast cancer for the Mom. Breastfed babies have fewer allergies, ear infections and, some studies say, higher IQ's and fewer incidences of obesity and hypertension. (3)

Lynn Lorenz (author of The Multiples Manual) says:

> Breast milk is the best food a mother can offer her newborn babies, especially if she gives birth prematurely. Breastfeeding for only a few short weeks provides health benefits, which can help protect babies from many diseases. Because there is no better nutritional value to be found, consider giving it a try. Gather as much information as you can, and give it your best shot. (6)

The difficulties of nursing multiples are obvious. It's a rigorous feeding/pumping schedule with little sleep; it is physiologically impossible to nurse all three at once; and milk supply varies from person to person in accordance with stress, psychological support, and physical well-being. General guidelines say that to produce enough milk for three is to add 500 calories per baby a day to your post-pre-pregnancy diet and pump or nurse around the clock every two hours. Is it possible, you ask? Can anyone attempt such a schedule? It is possible, and I have talked to many women who have done it.

Some mothers of multiples believe they prepare themselves up until delivery and feel confident that they taken all the necessary measures. However, once the babies are born they feel less clear and flounder for direction. "I wish I would have known more about what to expect after the babies were born," said Jennifer from Washington. She had read a lot about what to expect during her multiple pregnancy, but felt there was not a lot of post-delivery information available and, therefore, she was not as prepared when her BBB triplets were born.

Babies born prematurely may have difficulties with "latching on" and "nipple confusion." "Latching on" is the babies ability to attach to the breast successfully. A breast shield can help "latching on" by further extending the nipple to the babies mouth and giving them something a little more firm to feel. Nipple confusion occurs when babies who are given both a bottle and the breast simultaneously prefer the bottle. The bottle distributes the milk easier and faster with less resistance than the breast. If you are going to do both, ask your lactation consultant or health nurse about nipple styles that mimic breastfeeding.

One thought that had never crossed my mind during our pregnancy was that our babies would not go to full term. Being born prematurely at thirty-one and a half weeks, our babies did not have an ability to suck or swallow on their own for the first couple weeks of life. Without the suck/swallow reflex, the babies must be fed by an NG (nasal-gastric tube) making nursing virtually impossible until a bottle is introduced. Not everyone set of multiples regardless of what week they are born at has to have their babies go into to NICU (neonatal intensive care unit) to help develop their sucking and swallowing, but many do. It is noteworthy that 35% of twins and 85% of triplets are born before 35 weeks gestation, and many end up needing to spend some time in an NICU to develop skills usually acquired in the womb. (4) It's important to be informed, but it never hurts to hope for the best.

A premature baby usually stays a short time in the NICU. If the babies do have to stay in NICU, pumping breast milk is one of the only things you can do that no one else can. I'll never forget how great my sister-in-laws were while our three were in NICU. They came and stayed with me and drove me to and from the hospital to deliver my milk. They made sure I had enough water at all times and would support me in my decision to try to nurse, reminding me that this was my new full-time job, the thing I could do while the nursing staff and doctors at the hospital were doing everything they could do.

On pumping during her GGB triplets' stay in the hospital Meredith from Nebraska said: "I think, although time consuming, it was a fantastic way to start my kids off. Pumping during their NICU stay helped me feel like I was doing something for them at a time when you feel some-what helpless."

Once in awhile, I hear a nursing mom share a concern that if she nurses her husband won't have any bonding time with the baby. A few parents of multiples I talked to also felt this way, until they experienced first-hand nursing triplets. Ronatbi Yassine, a Dad from Aubi Dabi,

United Arab Emirates, who has BBB triplets, said: "I have some advice for all mothers, please breastfeed your babies. My babies are happier when their mother breastfeeds them." He and his wife worked out a schedule of nursing one while bottle feeding the other two. Helen R. from Missouri with BBB triplets said, "My husband, interestingly enough, has become the biggest supporter of the breast feeding. When I first told him I wanted to, he thought I was crazy. He said 'You know, well, how am I supposed to help you feed them?' It was a battle then, but about a month or two ago, when I wanted to quit, he was the one that convinced me to keep trying a little bit longer. I didn't expect him to become my biggest supporter."

Fathers can play a positive role encouraging breast feeding. Many moms of multiples shared stories with me about how their husbands supported them in their decision to nurse. It would seem counter-intuitive since it means less time for them to bond with the babies. Moms of singletons sometimes say their husbands complain that they don't get to hold the baby and feed them as much if they nurse. Perhaps because moms of multiples are usually pumping and nursing, Dads get a chance to still give bottles of expressed milk to the babies and so feel connected. Or, maybe it goes back to the fact that parents of multiples have waited longer to get their precious bundles of joy and in response try extra hard to make sure they get every possible benefit they can.

No matter how much you do or don't nurse, there's no question, there may be a tinge of guilt and perhaps unseen contempt from the outside. Often hospital staff and maternity nurses, just assume a mother will be breast feeding. New mothers especially may feel pressure from those around them to nurse or at least attempt to. One woman I interviewed said: "I thought when I quit nursing there would be a burning 'L' on my front lawn when I woke up." At first I didn't get it. Then she clarified; "You know a curse from the 'La Leche League.'" I laughed so hard I nearly wet my pants.

Looking back I can laugh now, but at the time when I was trying to juggle nursing all three, I did my share of crying. I did feel guilty, I was tired, but I thought it was the 'right thing,' as so many mothers do. I was unable to get all three to "latch on" completely and ended up nursing one at the breast while pumping for the other two. To this day my husband calls our daughter the "booby girl" because she was nursed exclusively. I chose to nurse her primarily because she had an apnea monitor and would stop breathing during feedings. I felt like if I nursed her at least I could keep a more watchful eye on her in case she stopped breathing. It was the recommendation of the doctor at the time but my husband claims by nursing her exclusively it didn't give him a chance to bond with her as much as the boys.

Remorse came later when I realized one of my sons was a habitual biter. Was it because he received his breast milk from a bottle and didn't get enough oral stimulation from nursing? Then I felt guilty about playing favorites. My older son was nursed for four years. All three of our multiples were nursed much less than for our first child. I was able to produce milk for six months for all three, and continued our daughter for another year. Nursing just one baby alone is not an easy feat. Nursing multiples is an order of magnitude slightly higher with the possibility that not all three will get equal mommy time. As moms we have choices and we have to do the best we can with what we have to work with. Friends and family need to be supportive and those with opinions of discrimination regarding nursing choices need to be ignored.

Desire alone is not enough to produce milk for three babies. In weighing the options of nursing or not, one may or may not have a choice. Many factors can play into one's ability to breastfeed whether it is just one baby or four babies. Not only can the babies have difficulties, but Moms can have problems as well. Engorgement, cracked nipples, fatigue, jaundice, lack of sleep, and depression are just a few examples of potential problems. Some problems are simply out of our control and we have to be able to let go of this.

I adopted a mantra of being a 'good enough' Mom early into our triplet's pregnancy, letting go of the 'exclusive-striving for perfection' Mom I had been struggling with for most of my teenager's life. No matter what one chooses, she is likely to experience opposition. Ultimately, one has to do what is best for her babies and herself and that may be breastfeeding, bottle feeding, or a combination of both. (3)

Support for breastfeeding begins at the hospital for some women. In our case a lactation consultant came to our hospital bed to help us make our decision and coach us along the way. I definitely would not have made it with out her. She got me an industrial strength pump and helped me set up my every-two-hour pumping schedule. She even purchased and delivered a "hands-free" bra for me to use so I could nurse and eat my meals at the same time.

Susan from Arkansas with GGG triplets was also successful at milk production and latching. She nursed all three exclusively for four months, but, due to lack of sleep and other circumstances, she weaned sooner than she had with her other three singletons. She said: "You know when they go to school they don't ask, 'Were they breastfed or were they not'? It's great for their brains. It's great for them; but if you can't, it's not going to hurt them the rest of their lives."

If you can, get connected with a 'mothers' of multiples' group; talk to someone who has successfully tried nursing multiples before making a decision either way. Breastfeeding is important, but keep the benefits in perspective. Children have a whole life time to learn healthy eating habits. Plenty of mom's breastfeed and brag about how great it is for their kids yet think nothing of driving through and picking up a "MacDonald's" hamburger on a regular basis. There are circumstances beyond our control and many horror stories people often like to tell expectant mothers. It may not be the first time you may want to consider the "good enough" Mom mantra and give up the "perfect" Mom fantasy. Let's face it; there really are no "perfects", except in JK Rowling's fictitious Hogwarts School of Wizardry.

I did if for five months. That was enough. I pumped and then I got the guilt when I stopped pumping. And I always had the guilt if I wanted to take a nap. My advice is don't feel guilty about that stuff. It's okay.

My other piece of advice is to buy the "Privet" (the hands-fee bra) if you are going to pump. You have to have the "hands-free-bra"...I got one for my friend down the street who was having twins.

Melanie F., Greenville, Texas, BBG

If it's important to you [to breastfeed], stick with it. If it's not important to you, don't worry or stress about it. Nobody told me 'Just stick with it; if you want to do it, you can. No one told me it takes three to four weeks for your milk to come in.

We did pumping in the beginning and one high calorie formula every other feeding. During the formula feeds I would pump then feed.

My youngest one didn't catch on until he was three months old, so he had only bottles until three months old and then he finally got the hang of it.

Jennifer M., Texas, GGB

Nursed all three until they self weaned at two years old

What the Experts Say
Common Problems and Solutions
Wendy Haldeman, MN, RN, IBCLC, The Pump Station, Santa Monica, California

In an interview with Wendy Haldeman, lactation consultant, at the Pump Station in Santa Monica, California. She offered several nursing tips for Mom's of multiples. "The earlier you get information (on lactation), the better chance you'll have of successful milk production," she said. Ideally, talking to the lactation consultant should happen prior to delivery. The morning I delivered our three kids, I had Corkey, the owner of the Pump Station, come to my bedside. She told me I would need to pump every two hours around the clock if I wanted to nurse all three babies. She also asked the hospital to deliver an industrial strength pump to ensure I would pump plenty. Fortunately she came by to consult with me because I had failed to look for a lactation consultant ahead of time. I owe her for being able to give the kids exclusively breast milk for the first few months.

Having nursed a singleton before, I remember the sort of generalized calm I felt with a let down of breast milk and I looked forward to this feeling with the triplets. This calm is an effect of oxytocin that is released when let-down occurs. But, I had forgotten about all of the cracked nipples and sore breasts in the first few weeks. Having the nipple cream helped with the cracked nipple problem. The sore breast problem was diminished because I used the pump regularly and therefore got less engorged than I did when I was trying to build up a mild supply for just one. The other item on the list, the hands-free bra, is a must when pumping for two or more. The bra looks like a cow utter holder but works like a charm when pumping.

According to Wendy, a mother of multiples should be pumping within twelve hours of delivery. "The sooner you are on the pump the better off you will be." The more the mother pumps, the more milk production; it is a simple issue of supply and demand. At first the mother will get what is called "colostrum" in very small amounts, and it's essential even though the mother might not feel as if anything is happening. I remember the nurses coming to collect my pathetic, little packages of colostrum and I thought to myself "is this really going to help?" But the nurses were always happy to see I was producing something. Our babies were in the mid-four pound range, so they didn't need a whole lot at first. At this colostrum phase, during the first three days, only this yellow stuff comes out and no milk. Whereas with a singleton, the baby at the breast sucked out this yellow stuff and made the mother feel successful, with triplets the mother must pump and notice this small production. Be assured it is worthwhile.

Wendy also pointed out that with a multiple pregnancy the placenta enlarges. For each embryonic sac has its own placenta, unless they are identical and share the placenta.   Since the placenta builds the milk supply and lays down the prolactin receptors that proliferate the milk ducts, the mother of triplets usually will have ample milk supply. The larger the placenta is, the more receptors available for milk production. However, the longer the gestational age of the pregnancy, the greater amount of time the placenta has to proliferate these ducts. So, early delivery may result in a lesser than ideal milk supply.

Another factor that can affect milk supply, said Wendy, is the babies' need for "betamethasone." Prior to delivery, the mother receives a shot of this drug to aide in the babies' lung development. Sometimes it is given at thirty-two weeks just in case of pre-term labor. Optimally, the mother would deliver within forty-eight hours of the "betamethasone" shot, but this is not something the mother may have control over. "If delivery is between two and nine days after the betamethasone shot, milk supply may be impacted negatively," said Wendy.

Some problems Moms' of multiples might have with nursing are low milk production or a problem with nipple preference. To help milk production, some lactation experts recommend pumping more. Other good ideas are to try relaxing and not letting outside stress interfere. Meditate, exercise, take deep breaths, soak in a tub, or take a few hours and spend some time with your friends – whatever you need to do to relax. Staying hydrated is also important. On average eight glasses a day of water. Eating enough is another important tip. Nursing moms need five hundred calories per child they are nursing above their recom-mended usual caloric intake (ask Wendy about this to double check). Some herbal suggestions are: mother's milk tea, fenugreek (three 590-61- mg capsule three times a day), blessed thistle (up to four capsules, three times a day), anise (crush one-to-two teaspoons of seeds into one cup of boiling water, drinking two-t-three times a day), alfalfa (four capsules, three times a day), and brewer's yeast (three-to-five tablets, three times a day).

When the baby selects the bottle over the breast, the baby may be experiencing a "nipple preference problem." The answer to this problem may be the introduction of a breast-shield. This is a plastic nipple that goes over your breast nipple to make the nipple firm and easy for the baby to get to. Once the baby latches on the shield is removed.

Some lactation experts, such as Wendy, feel that if you want exclusive breast milk, your best nursing mode is "tandem." In this practice the mother put two babies on her breasts at the same time. Obviously, with triplets the mother will have to rotate which two babies nurse at the same time while the other gets an expressed bottle. "There just aren't enough hours in the day to pump and nurse around the clock" says Wendy. She has seen many successful Mom's nurse tandem with their multiples.

Another possible reason some women may have trouble nursing according to Wendy, is that they don't "trust the breast as much as formula." Wendy reminded me that when the kids are in the NICU everything is measured and the babies' weight is closely monitored. Some hospitals don't allow the babies to come home until they reach a certain weight. Given the average gestational age of thirty-two weeks for triplets, many Moms of multiples are faced with pre-maturity and low weight issues. Any hospital practices that have an adverse affect on the mother's concern for her babies certainly will play a role her ability to produce adequate milk.

In a follow up conversation with Wendy she said some of her colleagues have babies going to the breast in the NICU as early as thirty-two weeks. When she and I initially spoke I shared how the NICU only allowed us ten minutes of touch times with our babies preventing nursing on the breast in the NICU. Other moms I interviewed said their NICU's were not as strict. These moms were more successful putting their babies on the breast sooner. So, be sure to work closely with the lactation consultant in your hospital and find out the parameters of visitation in your NICU. Nursing is a right of passage for any new mother and should not be denied because the mom has triplets.

Tips to Get Pumping

Tips to increase milk production:
- Pump or nurse often – at least every 1 and ½ to 2 hours per day
- Relax
- Stay hydrated
- Eat oatmeal
- Fenugreek – herb need to use more than 3500 mg/d to increase milk supply
- Blessed thistle – 3-4 capsules three times a day
- Drink "Mother's Milk" Tea
- Eat enough

Tips for pumping:
- Use a "Hands free" bra
- Rent or buy an industrial strength pump
- Purchase a large nursing pillow (for nursing twins)
- Use "Nipple cream" on breast and pump cup to aide lubrication
- Try olive oil or "Lansinoh" on nipples to prevent soreness
- Prop up feet with stool if feet don't touch the ground

My advice is to keep them on the same eating and sleeping schedule.
Karen B., Kenashaw, Wisconson, GGB

"A singleton mother cannot even imagine why mixing formula for three babies would be hard until you have to do it. Invest in the Pampered Chef Juice Pitcher. It is a lifesaver! I received it as a gift and was really thrown aback as to why someone would give me a gosh darn juice pitcher....now I know why. It was the best gift ever."
Jill A., Rochester, New York, BBG
BF 2/3 for one month

Our Surveys Said...

"What percentage of moms of multiples do you think nurse their babies?" I asked Jena T., a doula from Santa Monica. She said that she thought about ten-percent breast feed any of their babies at all. According to our web survey a surprising sixty-five percent of the mom's breastfed or pumped all three babies for three-to-four months. This revealing information about nursing multiples is inspirational and unique. The surveys showed that the number of moms who chose to breastfeed was higher than those who chose not to breastfeed. Two-hundred-and-forty-three responded "Yes" to the question, "Did you breastfeed?" One did not answer the question and another was still pregnant so couldn't answer. Of those who did breastfeed, ninety-three percent of them breastfed all three babies for an average of thirteen weeks or about three months.

The survey defined Breastfeeding as nursing at the breast or receiving expressed breast milk. Although in our survey demographics, ethnicity and age were not compared for correlations, the National Health Survey on Breastfeeding (1999-2006) indicated breastfeeding rates were greater among women with higher income and mothers who were thirty years and older (7).

Several interesting issues came up in the interviews. When appropriate I asked "Did the babies have breast milk only or a combination of breast milk and formula?" and "How often did the babies fed on the breast or through the bottle via expressed or 'pumped' milk?" The Moms who were successful with nursing explained that they succeeded by rotating; nursing one or two babies at a time, while the other one or two babies received a bottle of either "expressed" milk, formula, or a combination of breast milk and formula. Some pumped the other breast while they nursed with one whereas others fed two babies and then pumped after feeding to make more milk for the other baby or babies. Most pediatricians would agree that a combination of breast milk and formula is still better than formula alone since the goal is to give the babies the advantages of breast milk.

The trend to wean at three months was already documented in a 2001 National Immunization Survey on the prevalence of breastfeeding in the United States. The "exclusive" breastfeeding rate was fifty-nine percent at seven days and then drops to about eight percent at six months. The researchers reported that the number of babies being breastfed experienced a "sharp decline" between the ages of two and three months, the time when many women return to work or school and need additional support in order to continue breastfeeding. (5) These findings are very similar to those of the moms who filled out our questionnaires (2007-9). The Moms of multiples in our survey are to be commended for having just as high a breastfeeding rate as the singleton moms nationwide.

Nationwide more new moms are nursing now than over the past decade. But the push to nurse until six months of age hasn't changed. According to the National Health and Nutrition Examination Surveys from 1999-2006, breastfeeding rates in the United States has increased significantly between 1993 and 2006. The percentage of infants who were breastfed increased from sixty percent among infants born in 1993-1994 to seventy-seven percent among infants born in 2005-6. Although the rates of breastfeeding at birth increased, the rates of those women still breastfeeding at six months did not change. (7) So, even though the recommendation from the Canadian Pediatric Society, the American Academy of Pediatrics Section on Breastfeeding, and the World Health Organization is to breastfeed six months, the nationwide average is not in accordance with this recommendation. (1, 7)

How is it that Moms' of multiples are compatible with Moms of singletons in the length of time they nursed? Maybe, Moms' of multiples have bigger breasts? All kidding aside, there are a couple factors that may explain this exceptional behavior. Given the average weeks of triplet gestation (32 weeks) this usually includes an NICU stay of three-to-four weeks. Since Moms of multiples can't live in the NICU twenty-four hours a day, many Moms told me they pumped their milk while their babies were in the NICU in order to be connected to their little ones.

Seeing their babies struggling for each breath made this effort more doable.

Given that triplet babies are more often than not born prematurely, the small weight makes supply and demand easier to accomplish. If, for example, a Mom of a ten pound baby couldn't produce enough milk for him everyday, perhaps she could have if he had been only four pounds. Certainly a four-pound baby doesn't need to eat as much as a ten-pound baby. The lactation expert brought up a good point about placental tissue laying down more milk ducts. Since many of multiple pregnancies have multiple placentas, then perhaps the larger number of milk ducts helps Moms of multiples to produce more milk than singleton Moms.

Clearly it's not a matter of not being able to produce milk or not, if the majority of the women did indeed nurse or pump. The American Academy of Pediatrics suggests six months to a year of breast feeding. Maybe the amount of time is less than this recommendation because as the babies grow in size the amount of milk mothers can produce can not match the multiple babies demands. "Pump every two hours around the clock" was what the lactation expert told me at my post delivery bedside consultation. Somehow I was able to pump and nurse for the first six months. But looking back I see the effects of sleep deprivation had their consequences. The important message is: although Moms may have had trouble getting pregnant or difficulty carrying multiples to term, they may still be able to provide milk for their babies. It may not be the traditional way of nursing one at a time with the baby looking in your eyes and playing with your breast, but rotating between breastfeeding, pumping and giving formula can be a modification that best fits the circumstances. Many Moms of multiples did nurse their babies successfully for at least three-to-four months and that is note worthy.

STATISTICS

Percentage of Moms of Multiples who
Nursed and for How Long

From 252 questionnaires there were 243 valid responses our of which, 159 answered "Yes" whereas the rest answered "No" to the question "did you breastfeed?." This corresponds to a valid percentage of 65.432 percent (95% confidence interval for the portion of moms who breast-feed between 59.41% and 71.45%). Therefore, the number of moms who choose to breastfeed is statistically significantly higher than those who choose not to.

Among those 159 moms who breastfeed (or pumped), 147 of them, or 92.5%, did breastfeed (or pump) all three children. This shows that almost all the moms who choose to breastfeed (or pump) breastfed all three children.

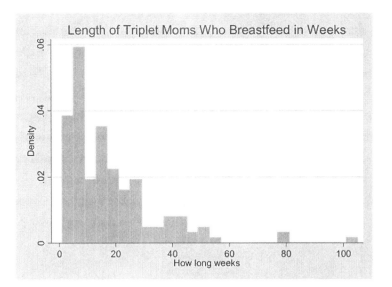

Among those 159 moms who breasfeed, 156 gave a valid response to the question "How long did you breastfeed?". The average length of time was thirteen weeks or about three months (95% confidence interval for average length of breastfeeding between 14.9 and 20.0 weeks).

Places to Get Help

International Breastfeeding Organizations
La Leche League International
PO Box 4079, Schaumburg, IL 60168-4079
Phone: 847-519-7730 or 800-LALECHE; fax: 847-519-0035
In Canada, phone 613-448-1842 or 800-665-4324
Email: llli@llli.org
Web site: http://llli.org/

International Lactation Consultant Association
1500 Sunday Drive, Suite 102, Raleigh, NC 27607
Phone: 919-861-5577; fax 919-787-4916
Email: info@ilca.org
Web site: www.ilca.org/

Australian Breastfeeding Association
PO Box 4000, Glen Iris, Victoria 3146 Australia
Phone: 61 3 9885 0855; fax 61 3 9885 0866
Email: info@breastfeeding.asn.au
Web site: www.breastfeeding.asn.au/

Bibliography

M. Boland. Exclusive breastfeeding should continue to six months. Paediatrics & Child Health_ Oct. 2005: 148

Breastfeeding can reduce a woman's risk of breast cancer. ACS News Center 19 July 2002

http://www.cancer.org/docroot/NWS?content?NWS

Fierro, Pamela. The Everything Twins, Triplets, and More Book. Avon, MA, 2005.

Gromada, Karen. Mothering Multiples. Schaumburg, IL, 2007.

Li, R., Zhao, Z., Mokdad, A., Barker, L., Grummer-Strawn L. Prevalence of Breastfeeding in the United States: The 2001 National Immunization Survey. Pediatrics 2003 May; 111(5 Part 2): 1198-201.

Lorenz, Lynn. The Multiples Manual. Pennington, NJ: Just Multiples.com, 2004.

McDowell, Margaret, Wang, Shia-Yih, Kennedy-Stephenson, Jocelyn. Breastfeeding in the United States: Findings from the National Health and Nutrition Examination Surveys, 1999-2006. NCHS data briefs, no 5. Hyattsville, MD: National Center for Health Statistics. 2008.

Personal Interviews
Wendy Haldeman, MN, RN, IBCLC
Karen Self

CHAPTER FIVE

. . . . .

Nightshift – How to Manage
Sleeping
Or
Lack There of It or Sea Legs

Kellie's Story

Kellie D. works as a consultant for an IT company in the child welfare field. She lives in Tallahassee, Florida, with her husband of six years. They have three girls from her husband's previous marriage aged 15, 12, and 10.

They needed help to get pregnant, so they tried IVF. They did one fresh round and then, four months later, one frozen round of IVF. They were told the chances of getting pregnant on a frozen cycle were less than the fresh cycle. "So, we were hoping to at least get one…and we got three." Not just any three, BBB triplets.

She carried the babies up to 35 weeks and 4 days. They only spent one night in the NICU for observation. The following two nights they spent in Mom's room. "So, while I'm trying to heal from, you know, the C-section and get used to not being pregnant, which my body didn't handle very well, I had three little babies". Kelly lost a lot of blood during the C- section and her blood levels were not where they needed to be. Her blood pressure spiked, and she needed medication to keep it on track. She had people staying with her, though and by six weeks it normalized. "My mom and mother-in-law were there for the first four weeks and then, we were on our own and have been on our own since."

When I caught up with Kellie the kids had just turned five months old. Laughingly I said – "Are you getting any sleep?'" She told me that they were sleeping all the way through the night (twelve-hour stretches) since twelve weeks of age. She said they take two really solid naps for about two hours a piece during the day and a little cat nap around dinner. "They're very good sleepers," she commented. "Wow", I retorted, "that's some schedule."

She had a good come back for me, she said: "Routine, routine, routine, not so much schedule; I have sort of set my mind on doing everything at a certain time. But it was really a routine of doing every-thing in the same kind of pattern of when they wake up, then they eat, then they play, then they sleep. You know, instead of a schedule, do a routine and the schedule will fall into place."

She admitted that the first two or two-and-a- half months were really hard. "There were times where the four–-me and the three boys, all four of us – just sat around and cried because I'm like, oh, I can't do it. But once we kind of fell into a routine, our day routine of getting their naps in on time, things just kind of fell into place. Night times were always pretty good for us."

I had to keep probing as to why her "Night times" were so easy. I asked "Do you have to coax them into going down, or keep them active or put them in front of the television, what?" "No," she replied. "I've never rocked them to sleep. They're held less. I remember our help hearing me saying, 'Put the baby down.' Ever since the help left, I've always put them down when they are awake, so they've always fallen asleep on their own. They don't know any different and now that they're older and there's time in the days, I can hold them and rock them. If I do and they're tired, it's almost like they squirm to tell me, 'leave me alone.' I'm like: 'No, cuddle with me.' And they are like: 'Just put me down cuz I need to go to sleep.'"

"It can't be that easy," I continued. "You must have some bedtime ritual." "Yeah, at night we do a nighttime routine of, you know, changing their diapers, giving them a little rubdown with lotion and putting them in their jammies. And by the time we do that, they're already starting to fall asleep. We struggle to even get them to take their whole bottle. I'm like, 'Wake up so you can finish the bottle.' So, when we put 'em down there's no problem."

"Any other secrets you care to share?" I pry further. She admits, "I have the most wonderful husband on the face of the earth. And, when I was pregnant, from the moment we found out there were triplets, any time I was home, he told me to just sit and rest and do nothing. He does pretty much everything around the house. He cooks, he does the grocery shopping. So all I've had to do was make babies!"

• • •

The triplets slept in the same crib together, swaddled in their own blankets until they were five months old. I believe this helped them sleep, and got them on the same sleep rhythm without bothering one another, even to this day.

From birth, the children awoke and slept at the same time, pretty flawlessly. Their synergy is amazing. Their three beds have always remained connected in some way ever since.

I long for the day when my daughter will agree to have her own room, but they just don't want to be apart, in fact they have a hard time sleeping sometimes when one of the others is not there.

These children really are an extension of one another, much in the same way we all are – they simply are born with an intuition of other human beings and retain that connectedness with one another that we as adults strive for.

Kelly V., Boca Raton, Florida, Six-year-old BBG

Sleep Training: Feberize, Baby Wise, or Improvise?

Sleep is one of the most precious and treasured gifts to parents with infants. Everyone has a word advice or stories of what they did or what they read about babies and sleep. Recently, the idea of sleep training has made front page news, although it is still one of the most sensitive child-rearing subjects. At the end of the day, parents seem to find that ultimate balance between what they think sleep is and what real sleep actually means. No right or wrong answers exist here. There are no good or bad sleepers. There simply is a time in every parent's life where they live with less sleep than they need.

Sleep training incorporates two extreme methods, suggests Tracey Hogg in The Baby Whisperer. The "Ferber" technique known as the "cry-it-out" method is at one end of the spectrum and the "Grin-and-bear-it" method of getting up from dusk-til-dawn as often as necessary is at the other. Somewhere in the middle of these is the "no-cry sleep solutions" that promote "baby whispering". In my interviews with Moms of multiples, it seems everyone has an interesting variation of how they get their babies to sleep through the night. Even my neighbor up the street, with eight-year-old triplets, stopped me last week and asked: "Are your kids sleeping through the night yet? Ours kids are still getting up and coming into our bed in the middle of the night." It is a hot topic for all parents, but strategies that work for families' with one infant may not be appropriate for families' with multiples.

With our three babies, the pediatrician recommended we begin to "sleep-train" them at six weeks. "Just put them in their cribs, say goodnight, and let them cry-it-out", she said. At our baby shower, we got three identical books on sleep training from three separate, well-meaning friends (On Becoming Baby Wise: The Classic Sleep Reference by Gary Ezzo and Robert Bucknam). Apparently our friends agreed with our doctor. The "Baby Wise" method suggests a "PDF or parent directed feeding" program which, if followed, supposedly trains your infant to sleep seven to eight hours continuously, as early as seven to nine weeks old. They use phrases such as "Don't be enslaved to your infant's unknown needs". At the time this sounded a lot to me like, "Ignore you poor, defenseless child's' needs." For some reason, my mothering compass did not point in the direction others were suggesting.

I just kept thinking to myself, would my pediatrician and friends recommend sleep training so strongly if I had just one baby? Nobody suggested any regimented sleep program with my older son, Tim. Thirteen years ago with Tim, I followed the Le Leche League guidelines of bed sharing or co-sleeping (having the baby in bed with us). One of the books endorsed by the Le Leche League, Mothering Multiples (2007), cautions about bed sharing with multiples due the risk of sudden infant death syndrome. They qualify their caution about this practice by saying it is not really a problem as long as the Mom is not on any sleeping medications, does not smoke, and is sober.

I fell into the same rut of trying to do for my three what I had done for my one, singleton child. Then, the reality sunk in that five of us may not fit into even the largest king size bed on the planet. However, maybe when they were infants, it could work for a little while. I talked to a Mom of eight-year-old triplets who had co-bedded her babies, (put them all together in one bed to sleep), when they were infants. She and her husband were both nurses, so they were aware of the risk factors. They followed all the guidelines for co- bedding such as laying the infants on their backs, lining up the heads together lengthwise, eliminating pillows or rolled up blankets between the babies, minimizing heavy coverings, and keeping swaddling blankets away from the babies' noses. After five months, she had to transition them into cribs, which she recollected as a little challenging.

My husband and I agreed that our three would be comforted at night, at least until they were two years old. I am from the group that believes that the only reason a baby cries is because he or she is tired, wet, or hungry. My husband Bill, (our resident shrink), feels there is another thing to think about. The baby may cry because he or she needs comfort or physical closeness to a parent. So, I lose a little sleep. How bad could it get?   Bill called my years of sleepless nights my "residency-training program." As a young resident in medical school he had many nights without sleep so he had no problem with me taking over this project as he would pop another "Ambien" (sleeping pill) in his mouth and sleep without being awakened by any of our children.

When the kids hit two years, four months, six days and twelve hours, I hit the end of my sleep deprived rope and "saw the light" literally by physically seeing less all together. I woke up and saw less of the entire room. It was like a black curtain on either side of my peripheral vision. Suddenly comforting their every whim took a back seat to taking care of me. The proper term is 'tunnel vision.' It is a neurological side effect of sleep deprivation.

Another problem with waiting as long as we did to give our kids the message that "Night-time is sleeping time" is because when they are old enough to walk and climb, the crib can no longer contain them. Our Jack was nick-named: "Jack-In-The-Box". He would pop right out of his crib and come into our bed in the middle of the night long after he had been "put to bed." One pediatrician was concerned about him breaking his arm. When I was sleeping on the floor, I could catch him in the act sooner and put him back into to his crib. But, my sleeping on the floor days were numbered, something needed to change. Several moms of multiples I talked to remedied this "Jack-in-the-box" phenomenon with a crib tent. A crib tent can be zipped over the entire crib and it helps to prevent the baby from crawling out. We did not try the tent with out kids, our solution was to hire a new ring leader.

When I finally couldn't physically do it anymore, my husband started putting the kids to bed. I have to say, if we had another set of triplets, I might consider sleep training sooner than two years. Turning over control to my husband did not come quickly and without reservations. For months I had tried to get them to sleep. I weaned the middle of the night bottles, watering them down at first. I tried variations of patting, singing, and picking up babies, all night long as I took up residency in the middle of their floor on an 'Aero' bed mattress. I made charts of who was sleeping and who wasn't and what my theories were. It is the crying I couldn't stand. It went against my intuition. Bill, on the other hand, could hear their cries and restrain himself from picking them up. He did not have the terrible guilt I had. After awhile, they got the message that Daddy was just going to sit in the rocking chair and keeping singing, no matter what.

I found comfort in the book, Healthy Sleep Habits, Happy Child, by Marc Weissbluth. He says, if children don't sleep all night and their sleep time is interrupted, they have more tantrums during the day. What do you know? Come to think of it, the one who was throwing the most tantrums during the day was the same one who was up two to three times each night. Not just mumbling in his sleep, but standing up in his crib shouting: "Pick me up Mommy, Uppie! Uppie!" Dr. Weissbluth also says; "Sleeping all night is a habit, it can be taught and, once learned, regression is unlikely, unless the kids are sick or the family goes on vacation, where the schedule is interrupted."

The final piece of information that helped sway our decision towards sleep-training was that statistics showed 95% of kids slept through the night by twenty-one months of age. Even adjusting for the two months of pre-maturity, our babies were still about five months overdue in regulating their sleep. Completely convinced, I turned over control to my husband, put on my _ipod_, went for a walk each night, blocks away from our crying babies.

A well known pseudo celebrity in our neighborhood is Harvey Karp, a Santa Monica pediatrician. People from all over the world take their babies to him to learn his methods. He is known as the "Baby whisperer". His book, 'The Happiest Baby on the Block', suggests that parents use baby-calming techniques which imitate the sensations in the womb – swaddling, side/stomach lying, shushing, swinging, and sucking. He claims that these techniques facilitate the "calming reflex". There's no arguing that he has proven, through his case studies, that incredible results can be achieved. One mother of triplets whom I interviewed said that her husband became a "Baby whisperer." Dr. Karp's methods worked great for them; in fact she was surprised how well this worked and claims that her husband could even "shush" the neighbor's kids to sleep.

These are just a couple of suggestions, but you do need to check with your doctor first as far as when you are able to start a sleep-training program. You may even want to try a combination of comforting-while tolerating a little fussing. Among those who filled out the surveys, stating that they sleep-trained, the majority of them began the program when the babies were eighteen weeks or four-and-a-half months old. Preemies may need to reach a certain age or weight before such a program is recommended.

With sleep, I definitely don't claim to be an expert, quite the contrary. I think we definitely failed in this department. It is one of the things I might consider doing differently given the chance. I most certainly don't want you to end up momentarily half-blind like I did. You might not want to wait to consider the advice of sleep experts as long as I did. What worked for us was a combination of being supportive and present, which includes singing or patting, while tolerating our child's distress as she or he learns a new behavior.

At two months old all three were sleeping a good eight hours during the night but during the day I kept them occupied by playing with them and getting to know their characters. At six months old I managed to get them into a routine and all three have their morning and afternoon naps together thus I have some time on my own.

Enjoy every moment-as they grow up fast. They are only small once. There will be good days and there will be bad days but try to make the most of it when you have good ones.

Amanda H., Malta, GGB

Synchronizing a Routine

A predominant theme in the section entitled: "Advice to other multiple parents," was to keep the children on a schedule and to stick to that schedule. Remember Kellie D. our lead off parent in this chapter? She recommends, "Start with a routine and the schedule will fall into place." To say "schedule" implies a time driven set of activities. What I think most parents are saying is that it is important to provide the children with a regular pattern of activities that is predictable day in and day out. Try not to fall into strict or exact measures of time. What is important is that one wants to try to get all three children doing similar activities together initially. In other words, if one baby gets up at six in the morning, then that parent should get the other two up at six in the morning so that they are all on the same morning waking routine. Many parents had a schedule of their own in place and it was that schedule that drove the routine to keep the kids sleep patterns normalized.

I didn't appreciate this advice until my kids started kindergarten. I always had one, Alex, who got up early. He was my "baker" because anyone who has ever worked in a bakery knows the work starts early. Every day at six o'clock we had our "mommy" time before the other two got up. At night, we had our "banker" Jack who went to bed at nine, instead of eight like the other two. He stayed up later, consequently, he got up an hour later the next morning, at nine o'clock. We teased him for maintaining "banker's hours". This seemed ideal; I had a little one-on-one time with him in the evenings when the other two were asleep.

With a newborn keeping me up every two to three hours and a new kindergarten program that started promptly at eight, my "banker" would have to go to bed earlier, which meant consequently that when my "baker" rose, so did the other two. I took the advice of many of the parents I had interviewed and re-started their routine from their infancy. Within three weeks, our big five-year-olds were going to bed together at the same time and getting up in the morning at the same time. As for our newborn, he has had the benefit of our lessons learned regarding sleep deprivation which have empowered us to keep him on a routine from day one. Maybe it's true what they say that some kids are just "good sleepers" and others are not. But, our last one is definitely the best sleeper. Maybe we are just too tired from our other three to hear him whimper in the middle of the night and that's why he sleeps through the night!

Whatever you do with your babies I hope that the decision you make, is one that you come to on your own, based on what you heart tells you, and not what others think is best. No one knows your babies like you do and the multiple mom mind set can be an extraordinary thing. Just remember to be comfortable with your decision and fins a system that works for you and your family.

Our girls soothed each other. The girls shared a bed until they were seven months old. One cried and the other gave her her fingers.
Jennifer S., Albany, New York, GGB

My advice to other parents of multiples: sleep- train your babies as soon as you can – keep them all on the same schedule.
Suzanne C., Hunterville, North Carolina, GGG Triplets

"I remember one night we thought, 'Okay let's just feed everybody on demand because what if somebody does sleep through the night and here are waking that one up all the time.' But, that ended up being a horrible night because we ended up being up all night. Everybody was waking at different times. We thought, 'Well that doesn't work!'"
Jodi G., Columbia Heights, Minnesota, BBG Triplets

My parents hired us a baby nurse for two weeks once a day, then we stretched it into three times a week for two weeks. The baby nurse said at eight pounds they should be able to sleep through the night. So, after four weeks one could sleep six hours. At twelve weeks, all were sleeping through the night. The best advice was from an OB nurse at the nail spa: "If they cry for five minutes it won't kill them!"
Shari S., Stamford, Connecticut, GGG

Stay on the NICU schedule!!!! Don't read too much into the stories on the internet.
Kathleen G., Stockton, New Jersey, GGG Triplets

Sleep-Training: Talking with the Experts
Jill Spivack, LCSW, Sleepy Planet, Pacific Palisades, California

Jill Spivack is a sleep expert from Pacific Palisades, California. She knows that parents have a difficult time letting their kids cry or work out their own method of self-soothing because she experienced this first hand with her own child. "I really want people to understand that when they come in for a consultation, read my book, or watch my DVD, that they realize, 'You're talking to the super supreme wimp of all Moms.' I got into sleep training because I had problems with my first child and I was the biggest wimp around the crying you've ever met in your life."

Jill and Jennifer Waldberger wrote the book The Sleep Easy Solution and have a company 'Sleepy Planet' (sleepyplanet.com). Both the book and the website can teach parents about the principles of sleep-training. Jill stated, "The goal of the book was to simplify sleep-training and the sleep process for parents and not make it clinical but rather make it reader-friendly and interesting." Jill's background as a social worker, psychotherapist, and sleep consultant has taught her to empathize with parents' experiences and anxieties. "The missing link in other books is a high level of sensitivity to how difficult this is for the parents to cope with. Sixty percent of the battle is getting the parents committed [to following through with the program]."

Good sleepers lend to happier well rested parents, there's no question about that. But the age old question is, "How do you get one, two, and three babies to sleep well and at the same time?" In the December 2009 edition of Time magazine, an article titled "The Year in Health – Highlights of the Past Year Where We Got a Lot Smarter," offers one of the supposed "break-throughs" of the year about sleep-training. The author, Jodi Mindell, describes information gathered from seventeen countries on nearly 30,000 kids from infants up to three years old. She found that "If you're rocked to sleep, nursed to sleep, fed to sleep at bedtime, you're going to need that every time you wake up." Her advice is to have the children fall asleep three feet away from a parent or care-giver. "If they're slightly separated, they sleep much better." This concept of letting the children soothe themselves to sleep, as opposed to swaddling, feeding or rocking them, can be found in many sleep training books and across many cultures.

Jill commented, "Sleep difficulties or sleep deprivation, or whatever you want to call it, is probably the number one parenting concern. It is something many parents experience with typical babies where the children just haven't learned to self-soothe, or how to get through the night without eating."

Timing for Initiating Sleep Training

I asked Jill about the ideal time to sleep train. She said, "Physically around four months is the earliest age we recommend for people to start a sleep program. We judge whether or not they are ready based on the level of weaning, whether or not they are nursing, and also by the level of crisis that the parents are in." I was fascinated and paused to think. Does it really depend on how exhausted the parents are? To what extent does it depend on the child's development? She clarified. "Ideally, you don't want to wait too many months, because at about eight months, then you have to deal with additional issues like separation anxiety and standing in the crib. [When] older children get beyond ten or eleven months, they start to test limits. They just don't want to go down. The ideal window is between five and eight months. But a lot of people at four months say, "We can't take it anymore!"

I explained to her that on our surveys we found the average age multiples slept through the night (with or without sleep training) was around four-and-a-half months. I confessed to her that I had made a mistake by waiting until ours were about two-years-old before weaning the middle of the night bottles. I also never followed the idea of putting them down while they were still awake so that they learned to self-soothe. I realized I had big problems! With our youngest son, we started a new routine at bed time n hopes of getting better results.

Also, Jill explained that there is a developmental reason for starting sleep training at an early age..."The ability to self-soothe comes around the time children go through a growth spurt in their brain. It is this growth spurt that will allow them to now remember how to self-soothe from night to night or even learn the process of self soothing. This happens typically around three months or four months. It is usually shown by the child being highly distractible, when they will pull off the breast or the bottle and look to see who's talking to them. Before you even think about sleep training, they must feel they are capable of doing so."

I suspected that this recommended age may vary for preemies who might need an "adjusted age." I asked Jill, if she knew about adjusting for developmental ages in babies born before full term and how she handled this. She said, "Yes, we always take into account pre-maturity. For example, for twins who are born at 34 weeks, we would expect 38 weeks as full term. So, at four months old for that particular set of twins, I'm going to deduct four weeks and say they are actually only three months old, and suggest that they are not ready to be sleep trained yet."

Creating a Routine

Once a parent determines the right time to "sleep train," certain steps should be taken. Jill states, "Our philosophy has seven basic principles. You have to address all seven of these principles the right way, in order to reduce your child's frustration in learning how to sleep and in keeping them on track with good sleep skills." We talked further about the various other philosophies, agreeing that self-soothing for the child is an important skill. As a consultant she listens to what the parents' preferences are, takes into account the environment, the children's association and the bedtime routine. I liked the acronym she gave: BEDS

B – Bedtime Routine: have a good bedtime routine

E – Environmental Factors: have a quiet environment without stimulation

D – Down Awake: child needs to learn to go down awake via self-soothing

S – Schedule: have the right schedule where the child is not over tired or under tired around their sleep or nap time.

Naturally there are times when keeping to the sleep training is not appropriate. When babies are cutting teeth, ill, or when you are traveling away from home, the routine becomes altered and parents' expectations need to change as well.

With regard to sleep-training multiples; often times one or more are good sleepers, but one out of the three may be a problem sleeper. One question that came up frequently in my interviews was, "Do you let the kids sleep together or separate them, when trying to train them to sleep all night?" Jill has experience helping parents of multiples sleep train and she commented: "Some of them are very successful staying together in the same room, and others need to be separated."

Jill recommends removing the "good sleeper or sleepers" and keeping the "troubled sleeper" in the room that is familiar to him or her. Parents say to the child struggling with his/her sleeping: "If you're not sleeping at night and you're yelling for mommy and daddy, we need to help you become a better sleeper. Your brother can't sleep while you're yelling, so we're going to move him into the other room for a little bit until you're doing better falling back to sleep." She says this is a motivator and it is not punitive, it is more rational and understanding.

One of the strategies for older kids who have anxiety or separation issues which Jill recommends is using "Mommy bears." These are stuffed animals the kids choose themselves and dress them and play with them to imitate Mommy. Ideally, the bears wear an article of Mommy's clothes. The personality of the mom goes into the bears by having the bears drive the car and cook dinner just like mom does. The kids have a personal book with a story about them having trouble with sleep and that these Mommy bears come to help them. Jill remembers a cute story about a mom of twins: They were three-year-old twin boys who were having trouble with fears at night. "I told the boys to go into Mom's closet and choose a piece of clothing for their bears." One of the little boys selected a bra for his Mommy Bear and walked around town with the Mommy bear showing off his Mommy's bra! It was so cute and it totally worked."

So, do whatever works. Mommy bears, pacifiers, even thumb sucking is acceptable if your children can get themselves back to sleep on their own. Parents can certainly be more relaxed when they have a good night's sleep themselves.

If I could do something differently, I would be more diligent about NOT rocking the babies to sleep. It is so difficult not to do this, but now that the babies expect it all of the time, how do you rock three tired babies at the same time???
Megan W., Oakfield, New York, BBG

I should have never put my daughter to bed with a binky!
LeAnn L., Brighton, Colorado, BBG

Our Survey's Said...

The survey asked "Did you sleep train the babies, yes or no? And, if yes, at what age did you sleep train?" The definition of "sleep training" was not given. It was an assumption that if the parents answered the question, they had some understanding of sleep programming as a systematic training schedule rather than sleeping through the night occurring coincidentally. Does this mean they all "let the babies cry it out?" In the follow up interviews parents elaborated more. In general, those that said they did "sleep train" started to put the babies down in a more awake state so the babies could soothe themselves to sleep and in the middle of the night and they stopped giving them bottles of formula or breast milk, offering water, a "binky" (pacifier), or a security blanket instead.

To my surprise, only forty-seven percent of the parents from our surveys implemented some sort of sleep-training program. Why the remaining fifty-three percent did not sleep train could be a number of reasons. Perhaps, by following the schedule from the NICU that the babies came home on the parents had no need to sleep train their babies. Maybe they always put them to sleep or to nap while they were fully awake and didn't use a bottle or any rocking method to put them to sleep. It may be that, perhaps like us, they just didn't want to force the sleep issues. After seeing them in the NICU and how fragile life is, it's understandable why it may be difficult to hear babies cry it out, especially if it is not only in stereo but surround sound times three.

Out of two-hundred-and-fifty-two responses, only one-hundred-and-fourteen (or forty-seven percent) said "yes" to the question, while the rest said "no" and thirteen did not answer the question at all. Less than fifty percent is not a convincing number. It is certainly no reason to go out and hire a night nanny, but by all means don't let that stop you if you want to have one. Sleep deprivation was rated third place in order of frequency in the section of the survey that asked, "What is the greatest challenge in raising multiples." "Establishing better sleep habits" scored sixth place in the section that asked parents if they had any regrets. I then went back and looked at all the parents who did not sleep train to see if they were some of the parents who commented that sleep deprivation was a problem and I found correlations only about one-third of the time.

Another section of the survey asked if there were "Any additional questions you would like answered?" This is where I would have filled it in and said, "How do you get them to sleep through the night?" Surprisingly to me, hardly anyone asked that question.

Of the forty-seven percent who did sleep train, the average age that parents started a sleep program for triplets was at about eighteen weeks. This seems to be on track with what some of the sleep experts say about when to have babies start trying to soothe themselves to sleep. Answers to the question of 'when,' ranged from zero to thirteen months.

• • •

At thirteen weeks they started sleeping from midnight to six in the morning. They slept straight through the night. You know once in awhile someone will wake up, but we either give 'em a bottle of water or their binky. Tiffani R., BBG

Sleep-train them as quickly as you can and get them all on the same sleep schedule. It makes life a whole lot easier. I would also say that even though the days seem to last forever, the years will fly by.
Joan G., Oakton, Virginia, GGB Triplets

STATISTICS
Sleep Training

For the question "At what age did you initiate sleep program?": There were 98 valid responses. The data values range from .14 week (or 1 day) to 56.33 weeks (or 13 months). The mean triplet age (in weeks) when the sleep program was initiated is 18.3897 weeks, with a standard deviation of 15.14 weeks.

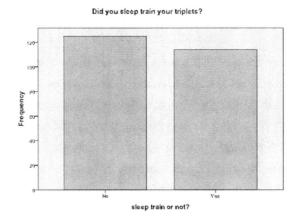

Bibliography

Ezzo, Gary, Bucknam, Robert. <u>On Becoming Baby Wise: The Classic Sleep Reference.</u> NEED CITY, STATE 2001.

Gromada, Karen. <u>Mothering Multiples.</u> Schaumburg, IL, 2007.

Karp, Harvey. <u>The Happiest Baby on the Block</u>. New York, New York, 2001.

Hogg, Tracey <u>The Baby Whisperer.</u> New York, New York, 2001.

Waldburger, Jennifer and Spivak, Jill. <u>The Sleep Easy Solution.</u> Deerfield Beach, Florida. 2007.

Weissbluth, Marc. <u>Healthy Sleep Habits, Happy Child,</u> New York, 1987.

Personal Interviews:
Kellie Darnell
Jill Spivack, LCSW "Sleepy Planet"

CHAPTER SIX

. . . . .

*Losing It – How to Get Rid
of the Prenatal "Buddha" Belly
Or
Dropping Anchor*

Laurie's Story

Laurie is an exercise physiologist/nutritionist with a Masters of Science degree in nutrition from Plainsboro, New Jersey. She works for a large insurance corporation as a manager in the Corporate Fitness Center. Her job allows her to do both managing and teaching in the fitness arena. On any given day, she may be instructing classes such as step, spinning and/or toning. Other aspects of her job include nutrition counseling or managing fitness clinics.

She is probably above average in regards to her personal fitness level and commitment to exercise for health and well-being. She is an advocate for life long fitness and, therefore, a good mom to spot-light for this chapter.

At the age of thirty-six, she gave birth to boy-boy-girl triplets. She had tried three rounds of IVF before having success in getting pregnant. She had a miscarriage at one point and was "benched" from being allowed to try again for three to four months. She remembers, "At that first ultrasound, there it was, clear as day, three sacks. And I remember my husband just smackin' his hands together and clapping. 'Well when it rains it pours! We're either not pregnant or real pregnant.'"

Because of the line of work she did and because she had maintained a high fitness level for many years prior, Laurie continued to teach exercise classes while pregnant with her three. She was able to continue these classes up until twenty-six weeks gestation. She has vivid memories of what it was like to teach exercise classes as a mom pregnant with multiples: "I was instructing aerobic classes until twenty-six weeks and continued with my personal work-outs up until thirty weeks. I really had a charmed pregnancy. I said to my husband that if I would have been pregnant with just one, I would have been teaching classes the day I gave birth. But, here I was thirty weeks pregnant, looking like I was going to give birth any day."

During the course of her pregnancy she had no back pain, pre-term-labor, or gestational diabetes. She also did not have to go on bed rest for a single day. She delivered her babies at thirty-five weeks, and they were in the NICU for only six days, for "growth." She commented: "Yeah, they were good-sized babies. I have nothing to complain about. The six days in the NICU were to help them gain weight and make sure they were eating well. We were really lucky."

At about four weeks post delivery of the babies, Laurie started back with a postpartum exercise routine. Within two months she lost the sixty pounds of "baby weight" she had gained in her pregnancy. She was able to return to work teaching classes after six months of leave. I asked her what her secret was. "I think teaching helped a lot. I do this for a living, that's the big difference. I do this day in and day out and I've been doing it since college for, my gosh, since college, thirteen years now. It's a lot of fun."

Being in the business of exercise and fitness for over twenty years myself, I have to agree that it has to be something you love or your just won't do it. But, with the addition of our three to our family, it's just so hard to make time for myself to exercise, eat right and stay fit. Laurie agreed, "I don't do anything competitive, especially now. Forget it. I don't have the time."

When I questioned her further, she had another good suggestion: "On the weekends I'm always exercising too, because I just love it." I said to her, "Well, I love it too, but I can never fit it in on the weekends." Then she laughed and said, "Now, on the weekends people laugh because they're seeing me with the triplet stroller. On my day off, when the weather's good, I'm out running, not with a triplet jogger, but a triplet carriage. My husband says to me, 'You know you can't attract enough attention walking down the street with three babies –no. You? You have to run. People must think you're nuts!'"

Laurie and her husband are fortunate to have jobs allowing them both to work either at home or in the office. They work a compressed work week.

She continued, "We're fortunate that our jobs have been so flexible for us. I work from home Mondays with a nanny. It's nice. She does the baby stuff so I can actually work, but I'm still here to see what's going on and hear what's going on, take a break and be with them. My husband is off on Tuesdays and it's daddy day. He takes care of them from five in the morning until I get home at four. Wednesday he works from home with a nanny and Thursday I'm off, so it's mommy day. Then again on Friday, my husband works from home. It's the best of both worlds. It really is."

A key factor in managing weight loss is a combination of both diet and exercise. Laurie has training in both areas. She commented about returning to her job as a fitness trainer and counselor; "It's not even like work. I do nutritional counseling for a lot of associates; more high risk people. Some have had heart attacks, heart disease, diabetes, high cholesterol, things like that; and, of course, obesity, that's a big one. I really love what I do so that's why I went back to work."

For some of us, it's what we do for a living, while for others it's how we chose to live our lives. All parents of multiples know that we are three times more responsible for setting a good example for our kids. They will get their food and exercise habits from us. Having an exercise program for yourself is a lot to manage when the kids are little, but if you follow Laurie's lead and just take them along, they'll get the message.

• • •

I have lost 120 of the 130 pounds I gained, but it has taken three years or so. I used Curves three times a week and exercised with students in school once or twice a week.
Kristi W. – Physical Therapist, Leslie, Michigan, BBB

Natalie gained 45 pounds and lost all of her baby weight in 6 months. She was a high risk pregnancy, so she couldn't do any prenatal exercise classes, but after the babies were born she walked everyday and pushed the triplet stroller. She said, "They loved it and I was able to exercise." Natalie W. , Pierce, Nebraska, BBG

Marie lost all of her eighty-five pounds six months post-delivery by "chasing children."
    Marie J., Round Rock, Texas, BBG

Will I Ever Lose This Weight?

Just hours before I delivered our triplets I remember e-mailing my brother a picture of myself. It was like the shot of Demi Moore in <u>Vanity Fair</u> years back when she was naked, standing sideways with a towel around private parts. The difference between her shot and mine was about a hundred more pounds and an IV. I asked my brother, a seasoned father who watched all three of his kids being delivered, what he thought. He was speechless. "It was too painful to look at you!" was his response after a long pause. Throughout the pregnancy I just couldn't stop wondering if I would ever get my body back?

My concerns were simple: "How big *was* I going to get? Would it be painful if I got too big? How would I lose the weight while caring for three babies at home? And, finally, how long would it be before I had my trim shape back?" After hearing the stories of other moms of multiples sharing their strategies of belly-recovery and life-long fitness, my concerns were put to rest. I no longer worried about taking residency at every "Weight Watchers" meeting from Santa Monica to the Pacific Palisades.

I apologize ahead of time for focusing on such a trivial topic. There are so many more important aspects of a high-risk pregnancy to concern oneself with than one's body image. Call it vanity or naivety. I asked other moms of multiples many questions about their weight gain and loss. Thankfully they obliged. One mom actually thought we should put a whole "Tummy wall of fame" in the book portraying the best and the worst abdomens! Fortunately moms of multiples have a good sense of humor.

The Pressure to "Lose the Weight"

My pressure to lose my baby weight came from living in an area inhabited by skinny Moms. Here in West Los Angeles, breast jobs and tummy tucks are purchased as often as patio furniture. It doesn't help that every checkout stand in the supermarket has magazines where the front covers are devoted to "Who's getting their body back in shape after their baby?" Writing about Heidi Klume, to Jennifer Garner, Nicole Kidman, or Octo-mom, reporters make a living exposing how these famous moms "did it." I understand many of these famous women have to get in shape and stay fit because, as actresses and models, it is their profession. Inadvertently in Los Angeles, I compare myself to them, even though I know I shouldn't.

There's more than one way to get back in shape. Unfortunately many moms do it the wrong way to try to accelerate the process. In a poll of post partum moms, 61% said they would either skip a meal or avoid family meals to lose weight. About 45% stated that the pressure came from within; they really wanted to be slim again. (5) Maybe the media plays a role or maybe we are internally driven to accomplish this. If it is unavoidable and inevitable, maybe the focus should be on how it is possible.

How did you lose your weight?

Simultaneous diet and exercise are necessary for permanent weight control. Successful moms of multiples who lost all of their baby weight agreed that it was necessary to eat right and exercise in order to get the weight off and keep it off. Answers about weight loss from the moms varied from organized national programs such as "Weight Watchers" or "Curves" to self guided exercise programs such as taking the babies for a stroll every day. The Moms offered many creative answers including "hooping" while watching television with the kids.

Theresa lost all of the thirty-three pounds she gained in four weeks. She did it by exercising – walking and running. She had no back pain during her pregnancy or gestational diabetes.

Theresa H., Naperville, Illinois, GGG

It took Natalie six months to a year to lose all of her baby weight. She gained forty-five pounds.

She worked out up until the day she found out she was expecting her trio, at twelve weeks. Then, she had to go on bed-rest at twenty weeks for about eleven weeks.

Natalie B., Dade City, Florida, BBG

Guidelines for Post-Partum Rehabilitation: Six Steps to Success

1. **Exercise with a buddy or a group:** Group classes or exercising with a friend combine the psychological social benefits with physical benefits. Eighty percent of people will stick to an exercise program if they do it with a buddy. (14) "Mommy and Me" groups have instructors who are usually moms themselves with plenty of good advice. Melissa Morrill, owner of Natural Lullabies, offers a "Mommy and Me" yoga class for mothers with children ages two and younger. She says, "The class gives the moms an outlet beyond the feeding/diaper changing/sleeping schedule, and some emotional support. A lot of good friendships are made here." (1) The challenge for moms of multiples is finding the time to squeeze the exercise into the new and busy lifestyle.

In order to make time to exercise use every opportunity that comes along. For example, if someone offers to help, ask them to come at a time when there is a "Mommy and me" yoga class offered and bring one baby along with you while your helper stays home with the other two. Maybe someone in the family can splurge and send a trainer to your house once a week for a couple months. Or, maybe a girl- friend will come and exercise with you while you both manage the kids together.

Be realistic with your exercise design. Getting out will be more difficult but that's not to say you have to skip exercising all together.

2. Training Specificity – Train both Power and Endurance Muscle Types: Training specificity is performing exercises appropriate for the muscle type, aerobic (endurance training) or anaerobic (power training). A balanced fitness program involves training both power and endurance type muscles. Different muscles in the body are responsible for different actions. Anaerobic muscle fibers are responsible for strength and bulking (or skimming the sagging parts), and aerobic muscle fibers help develop endurance for the long days of child-care. Since aerobic and anaerobic muscles perform different functions, it is not always possible to train them simultaneously. A possible work out design is to do weight training on Tuesday and Thursday and do aerobic exercise the other days.

3. It Takes 12 Weeks To Build Muscle and Flatten Flab: When one performs anaerobic exercises, such as working with weights, the muscles get firmer and usually more defined; this is called hypertrophy. Hypertrophy of muscle occurs when the bulk of the muscle increases in response to proper training. Muscle hypertrophy of any muscle in the body takes twelve weeks if exercised at least two twice a week with a proper training schedule.(6) Those are the minimal guidelines for all anaerobic training programs. Of course, anyone can exercise her muscles every day instead of twice a week, but it won't necessarily speed up the rate of hypertrophy. It may affect the amount of hypertrophy. (2, 3)

If an anaerobic program stops for two weeks or more, then all of what has been gained will be lost and the individual must start from scratch again to try to build muscle. Any interruption such as a two-week vacation or three kids sick with the flu one after the other, means back to the starting gate. To recap: exercise with weights at least twice a week for a minimum of twelve weeks without any more interruption than two weeks and a flatter tummy should appear.

Anaerobic contractions are exercises with weights or some sort of resistance. They are exercises performed with short bursts (one to three seconds) of excursion at maximum strength. Nady Suleman (also known as Octo-mom) says, "I won't work out without weights. That's my huge secret. If you slim down with cardio, you have to build muscle to replace the fat. Otherwise it would all just be hanging skin, and I wouldn't want that!" (4) It is difficult for anyone to maintain a regular program when they can't see results immediately. Try not to get discouraged at minimal progress, because it takes three months before any toning will occur.

4. Endurance Training – Pacing is the Secret

Aerobic exercise is such that ideally it is done continuously for at least twenty to thirty minutes with a targeted heart rate at sixty-five to seventy-five percent of maximal rate. A way to calculate an individual's target heart rate is the formula 220 minus your age times sixty-five or seventy-five percent. Many fitness machines such as the "Stairmaster" or treadmill have charts where these target zones are mapped out. Endurance contractions are the longer contractions that need to be at "sub-maximal" effort to ensure less fatigue. The endurance part of the muscle must be trained differently than the power portion of the muscle. Contractions at full force will die out quickly, while contractions at mid-range effort can be sustained for longer.

A common mistake when beginning an exercise program is pushing too hard, too soon. Moms of multiples have to be especially careful to keep from getting injured because they have to be fit enough to meet the demands of their little ones. An ideal cadence in a beginning walking program is to be able to walk and talk. In order to train for endurance, "sub-maximal" contractions must be performed. If talking is labored, then the effort is more than "sub-maximal" and the heart is working too hard. If muscles become fatigued because they can not maintain the demand it could lead to injury. Even moms of singletons need to listen to their bodies, if they want to develop long term wellness. Jennifer Garner's trainer, Valarie Waters says that Garner's workout mantra is simple, "Kids before cardio. 'If the baby didn't sleep well one night, then the next morning we might go twenty minutes instead of sixty." (11) You don't have to be an actress or rocket scientist to know to listen to your body and pace yourself. Only you know what sort of a sleep you had the night before so do what you can when you can because you can't buy sleep at the market.

What Is Wrong with my Belly?

Here's a clip from one of my website columns.

Dear Julie,

I have a large belly from the birth of my triplets. If I lie down flat and lift my head, it's like a "pop-up-tent" and I can put my whole fist between my abdominal muscles. The kids are almost four now, and I just can't seem to get rid of it. I've used a personal trainer, but he says he can't give me any abdominal exercises because I have a "hernia" or large protruding belly.

It was so embarrassing the other day. I was at the swimming pool and one of the little girls my daughter was swimming with came up to me and said: "Are you having another baby?" I tried to brush her off and said, very politely, "No". But, you know how four-year-olds are. She went on to say: "Well, then why is your belly so big and body so small?" Please help!

Big Belly Mama in Texas

Dear Big Belly Mama,

What you have is known in the PT world as a "Diastasis Rectus Abdominous." In my experience as a physical therapist who specializing in Women's Health, this condition is transient and can be improved with proper exercise and without surgery. It occurs when your Rectus Abdominus muscles go East and West to make room for the unstoppable, growing uterus.

Sometimes, in pregnancy you'll notice a black line (linea negra), running down your abdomen, and that is the beginning tell-tale sign that the hormones have begun to mediate the split. There's a nice online video you can watch on "beauty.expertvillage.com/videos/pregnancy-exercises-diastasis.htm" that explains the parameters for exercising.

It sounds like you have a five-finger split if you can put your whole fist in your belly. Your trainer should know that to exercise without addressing the split is not recommended, but, if you brace it properly, you can work on while safely narrowing the gap. One thing that will help when you're doing vigorous exercise (running or tennis) is an abdominal binder. I recommend the "Betterbinder" by Trenna Wicks.

I also suggest you go to www.womenshealthapta.org and go to "consumers" then click on Women's Health PT Locator and do a search by state or select the specialty area you are looking for (i.e. pregnancy postpartum). That is the American Physical Therapy Association home page. If you look under "Find a PT" and enter your zip code, you can scroll down to "Women's Health" specialty and find an OB/GYN Physical Therapist in you area who can help you.

I have used kinesiotaping over the diastasis, counter-bracing exercises or electrical stimulation in the past for this condition. If you have any trouble, write back to me and I'll help you.

You don't have to live with this condition. I've seen women reduce an eight finger diastasis to a two finger (which is normal), so don't give up hope. It can get better.

Thanks, good luck
Julie

5. Exercises to Correct a Diastasis Rectus Abdominus

A Diastasis Rectus Abdominus is a split of the abdominal wall muscles. It is common in women who have had a particularly large abdomen during pregnancy. To test for one, lie flat on your back with your knees propped up, and lift your head slightly. This position flexes the rectus abdominus muscles (or six pack muscles). If there is a cavern in the middle that stretches more than two fingers wide, a diastasis exists.

Anything more than a two finger split requires bracing. The "Betterbinder" is a good brace for this condition.

Exercises to lessen the spit of the abdomen muscles are as follows: Start back-lying with knees bent. If the abdomen can tolerate pressure from your hands, then use both hands crossed over one another in front of the abdominal wall to approximate or pull together the split in the middle. Maintain pressure while performing abdominal wall exercises. If pressure of the hands on the abdomen can not be tolerated, an alternative method of maintaining abdominal muscle closure is using a sheet wrapped around the waist. The sheet is folded in the width several times and then wrapped around the waist lengthwise. Cross the sheet in front of the abdomen with each end held by a separate hand, pulling it across in an "X" fashion while performing the abdominal wall exercises.

Abdominal exercises include standard sit ups and diagonal sit-ups. Basic abdominal wall exercises are recommended: lift head, elbow to knee, and knee to chest or leg slides. Leg slides are done by sliding one leg up to the hip by bending at the knee while back-lying. Once leg slides have been mastered, single leg lifts can be added. Double leg lifts are too forceful and should be avoided in early programs. As muscle tone and strength improves do mini abdominal crunches when reclined or sitting on a cardio ball.

6. Don't Forget the Bottom of the Box

The pelvic floor muscles are often forgotten when planning an exercise routine. All women need to exercise their pelvic floor muscles for feminine health. These muscles are located at the "bottom of the box" so to speak, when discussing the core stabilizer muscles. The front part of the box is where the transverse abdominus muscles are located. They can be felt by placing one's hands on their front pelvic bones and pulling the belly-button in. These tightening bands of deep muscles in the abdomen are frequently discussed as the core training muscles.

There are two other sets of muscles which are just as important as the transverse abdominus. In the back of the box, the multifidi of the spine are located, while the bottom of the box is made up of the pelvic floor muscles. These bottom muscles are frequently ignored. All three work together to hold the organs in place and act as a fibrous corset aligning and stabilizing one's "core." The back muscles will come on without having to separately recruit them. The pelvic floor muscles, on the other hand, need selective recruitment. If one doesn't activate her pelvic floor muscles the muscles may not turn on or they may get stretched.

Pelvic floor muscles, although invisible, can be felt when one tries to stop urine midstream or attempts to keep from passing gas. If one curls their toes like for picking up a marble, automatically the pelvic floor muscles contract. These muscles should be activated several times during the day for quick contractions and slow, twenty second contractions. "Wink your eye, wink your anus," I say half joking to my clients, but that's how fast a quick contraction of the pelvic floors needs to be. For a slow pelvic floor contraction, one way to describe the movement is to think of a straw coming out of the top of your head and imagine that you are a milkshake being sucked up that straw. Do them at stop lights or when waiting in line. Slow contractions should be performed when one can focus on their breathing as well as their movement. I usually recommend patients do them in the early morning or late evenings when things are a little quieter. Do five or ten slow contractions for a hold of twenty seconds twice daily. Think about being in an elevator and trying to keep from passing gas is another cue.

Carolyn was on 'modified bed-rest' at twenty weeks per the doctor's orders. She remembered, "That meant I worked from home in a recliner with a laptop and phone, and did less activity than I normally would."

It took Carolyn one year to lose her entire baby weight gain of one hundred pounds. She stayed as fit as she could before she was put on bed-rest by swimming and walking in the pool and light stretching. Post-pregnancy she did a lot of walking, some work-out classes and a little bit of hiking.

Carolyn M., Phoenix, Arizona, 17 m/o GGB

"I was in excellent shape prior to the birth [of her three boys], I had run a marathon the year before. I have jogged and gone to the gym but I still have thirty out of the fifty pounds I gained to get off."

Jennifer N., BBB

What the Expert's Say

Exercise Expert, Deena Goodman, PT, WCS, BCIA-PMDB, West Los Angeles, California

Deena Poll Goodman, PT, WCS, BCIA-PMDB is a board-certified specialist in Women's Health physical therapy, and is in private practice in West Los Angeles. She draws on her training in nutrition science, psychology, and Integrative Body Psychotherapy techniques that she incorporates them into her practice. I interviewed Deena for tips on post partum belly flattening. I asked her what she does to promote weight loss for someone who gave birth to multiples. She gave me some new information about "Smart Bells," "Hoops," and some old information about cardio and breathing to boost the endorphin levels.

I thought she would be a better advocate than me because after two kids she really is a walking example of fitness. Don't get me wrong, I'm just as strong an endorphin junkie as the next sports-minded PT, but I'm no where near the level of fitness that Deena is. I still have about five, okay maybe ten (as I shove another meringue cookie in my mouth) more pounds to go from my pre-triplet weight. But we both agree that it's not just the number of pounds, but rather, the shape we hope to get back. Yes, I need to lose the pounds and stop eating these high sugar content meringue cookies, but I could deal with a few more pounds if I could only lose this saggy, wrinkly belly. She commented, "When people say 'lose the weight' they are not necessarily talking about losing pounds, they are talking about the physical shape of their body."

I first asked her what she thought the number one problem is when moms of multiples start trying to get back into shape. "Is it uniquely different than singletons when they are rehabilitating?" I asked, "Is it the 'Diastasis' or muscle separation from a largely stretched out abdomen that is the primary problem?" Deena did not think the "diastasis' was the number one problem (even though she knows it is a problem) but rather something more simple to fix. "I think that the number one difference [between moms of multiples versus moms of singletons] is that they tend to get less 'cardio' believe it or not. You would think they would be getting more 'cardio' but – quite honestly – they often times are getting less cardio because they are homebound [after delivery] for much longer than moms who have singletons. There is also a tendency for them to be less active during their pregnancy because of bed rest restrictions."

Sometimes I hear moms comment on how their kids keep them busy all day and they feel that's exercise enough. However, she explained, "Sure, they are getting more activity because they are changing more diapers, and are moving around more because there are physically more bodies in the house, but that doesn't equate to the 'cardio' level you want for mental or physical health, or for taking off excess pounds. Yes, I think the abdominals are a big piece, but I wouldn't say it's always the diastasis that gets in the way. Often times they are getting less 'cardio,' if you compare them to the singleton moms."

So, if it is as simple as just getting more cardiovascular exercise while being homebound I wondered, "What is the solution?" Deena had a creative answer. "I look at my clients and think; 'What can moms do around the house, if they are homebound, that's going to give them a little more cardio?' Sometimes they'll even have a spin bike, right? Maybe it's in the garage.

Also, something to get their heart rate going would help the cardio. Up and down the stairs twelve times to get a burst in their heart rate, [for example]. A little bit of endorphin release also helps with depression."

The cardio ball or "Swiss ball" is one of my favorite pieces of exercise equipment to have when babies are small. Any Mom can bounce her kids on the ball if they are fussy and entertain them if they are bored. She can put one on each lap. When bouncing on the ball, the mom is working more of the pelvic floor muscles which are great for overall feminine health, especially post partum. Deena agrees but feels that sometimes mothers of multiples post partum may need a little more support while bouncing on their cardio ball. "I look at what they can do with their arms and feet at the same time. Bouncing on the Swiss ball – working abs [abdominal muscles] should be done in a way that's going to protect and support the back and the pelvic floor. They may need to have 'that belt' for a little bit longer to give a little more support while they are working their abs."

The type of brace she is referring to is the "Trenna Wicks Belly /binder" support brace. It is a little more specific than an abdominal binder and supports from below to distribute pressure away from the back and sacro-iliac joints located at the base of the spine. She continues, "This way when they are just working around the house they are also holding their abs in better alignment while doing household chores [or lifting babies in and out of cribs]."

The next important component of rehab that Deena discussed was breathing exercises. The ones she describes were unfamiliar to me in me, but sounded similar to yoga. Deena was not keen on recommending the practice of yoga as a general guideline for post partum rehab because of the high incidence of ligamentous laxity from high levels of pregnancy hormones and therefore predisposition to injury. Here's what she says: "The second thing I do is breathing exercises. Getting them to do something that changes their nervous system a little will make them feel better. If they are really overwhelmed they are, often times, not feeling as grounded and can use some physical coping strategies to help balance the connection of mind and body." She adds, "The types of exercises I recommend help to integrate the left and the right brain – 'left-right brain integrative breathing exercises.' It makes them feel a little more grounded in their bodies. There are a wide variety of breathing exercises. You have to find what works for you. It's based on the principles of Hatha yoga. The chest breathing exercises which energetically charge the body are quite different from than the belly breathing exercises which tend to be more calming to the nervous system. I tend to use the belly breathing one more [with moms of multiples] than I do with singleton moms."

Since I was unfamiliar with these exercises I asked her to elaborate more. "Basically when you do chest breathing – which is different than diaphragmatic breathing – different patterns and sequences give you more blood flow and more oxygen and that's what you're trying to do. It's about getting a sense of well-being in your body." She goes on, "When you are always thinking about your kids, the groceries, etc., and overwhelmed, you're not grounded, not in your body. There are different exercises to get people grounded. These are the kind of exercises that can make your meditation better, if you do meditation. If you oxygenated well before you meditate, then your meditation may be more fulfilling."

Finally, Deena recommends exercises to improve the inner muscles of the body, or stabilizers-the multifidi, transverse abdominous, and pelvic floor muscles. The term "Core" muscles is the more popular vernacular that tends to be thrown around in fitness clinics, but Deena and I agreed that is too vague a term. She goes on, "I don't like using the word 'core.' It's about using the muscles in their bodies that they can't actually see. That's where our expertise [as pelvic floor therapists] comes in handy. It's especially important for moms of multiples because they're often doing activities repetitively; so they're more prone to injury."

Deena divulged another secret. "You are not going to get a firm belly by doing regular sit-ups. I use 'Smart Bells.' They are fabulous! There is a whole series of exercises that can be done to really addresses connecting and using the pelvic floor; they are great for training the deeper muscles they are great." She goes on, "It's fun. You can use the weighted bell and do all sorts of fun moves. It's more about movement than it is about repetitive positions to do abdominal work. You're really working your back and your upper body and everything all together."

"Another possible way to firm the belly in a creative way with your kids in tow is hooping. There are hula hoops in different weights and sizes. These are not the kind one would buy at 'Toys R 'Us.' They are specially handmade for hooping." Deena confided more, "Absolutely, I actually hoop. We have hoops in our clinic, and I do group hoop session in the park and incorporate them into my one on one physical therapy sessions with moms. It's one of my favorite social activities with girl friends, and my patients love it too! It's fabulous to help get your shape back." Deena says, "You build up a sweat doing it. Don't forget to 'change it up.' The heavier the hoop, the easier it is, and then you use different muscles. Also, make sure you go both directions."

The key to any exercise and diet program is in making healthy lifestyle choices. Everyone is motivated by different factors. For some, having a partner to work out with is helpful: either your spouse, your friend or your kids if you're jogging them around in your triplet jogging stroller. The next time someone asks if they can help out, ask them to come over and watch two kids while you stroll with one so that you can boost your cardio and your endorphins. It's hard to walk fast if you're trying to push three kids in a big stroller. Think about what motivates you. Whether it's "Hoops," or "Smart Bells," or just getting an old spinning bike out of the garage, it's time to get moving. Your kids won't wait for you to catch up to them once they hit the ground running. They need parents who can keep up!

Medical Nutrition Therapist, Dorothy Bernet, MS, RD, Healthy by Design, Santa Monica, California

Dorothy Bernet counsels post partum moms on restoring their original weight and maintaining long term weight loss. She is the co-founder of "Healthy by Design Nutrition Specialists," a diet and wellness clinic in Santa Monica, California. She and her colleague, Stacey, work to help clients get on track with healthy eating. When I met with Dorothy, she shared her tips about starting a post partum weight loss program. She looks at an individual's overall lifestyle, recommends keeping meals simple, and asks her clients to keep a food journal. In this interview she explains why it may be difficult to get back on course to eating in a healthy and elaborates on keys to long term success.

When Dorothy first sees a client, she looks at the person's overall lifestyle and food habits. She told me, "The first thing we do is look at what the clients are doing as far as a typical day? How often are they eating? What are they eating? Are they snacking? And, what are they choosing to snack on?" In their food journal they record not only what they are eating, but what activities they are doing and what events happened during that particular day. Having worked with Dorothy many times over the course of the past two years, and being a veteran of "Weight Watchers," I know first hand how helpful this process can be. My journal doesn't lie, unless I don't record in it accurately.

With moms of multiples many factors make weight loss programs challenging. "How are your recommendations different for a mom of multiples?" I inquired. Dorothy says, "Be realistic. Look at your lifestyle. Do you have help in the kitchen or is taking care of the babies and preparing meals all on your shoulders? If it is all on your shoulders, you have to keep the meals simple and easy. You are not going to be going to the Farmer's Market twice a week and creating gourmet meals."

Dorothy and I talked about meal preparations and short cuts to meal planning. In the first few months when the kids started school, I experienced daily panic attacks at four o'clock because I wasn't sure what to make for dinner. I grew to appreciate the importance of being organized. Planning something healthy is always a struggle for me. Dorothy recommends, "Keep the meals real simple and plain, grilled or baked foods with whole grains, steamed or sautéed veggies. Stir fry is really easy. Look at your plate; on it you should have your protein, your starch and lots of veggies." She continues, "The veggies will help with the weight loss. The more you can fill yourself with what is healthy, the more easily you can get your body back into shape."

A pitfall many moms stumble into is an urge to grab comfort foods. Some moms even confessed, "I sneak and eat potato chips when the kids aren't watching." Dorothy explains why sometimes we search for the wrong answers. "Women in general love carbohydrates; they really do. It changes or raises their serotonin levels. Serotonin is a neurotransmitter thought to be involved in mood regulation in the brain. Certain food can be comforting. It makes us feel good. Breads and pastas and those kinds of foods are comfort foods." Not only comfort, but energy, she explains, is the reason we sometimes crave the wrong foods; "Moms of multiples are looking for energy where ever they can get it, and often times they'll go straight to the fast energy boosters, sweets and sugar."

Three Keys to Success for Permanent Weight Loss
1. Keep a food log
2. Exercise every day
3. Eat a healthy breakfast

Dorothy shared key factors to long term weight loss: "The National Weight Control Registry is an organization that keeps track of people who have lost thirty pounds or more and kept them off for at least a year." I had never heard of this registry before. Apparently, in the registry, thousands of people are recorded. From time to time they are interviewed and surveyed. Dorothy continued, "According to this registry, there are certain factors that really make a difference in your success." She had my attention. "One is keeping a food log. Some people have been in this registry for many years and they continue to keep a food log.

It keeps you honest. Assuming you are going to be honest in it."

The next essential item on the list (according to the National Weight Control Registry) is exercise. Dorothy reports, "They recommend exercising thirty minutes everyday." When Dorothy and I discussed common problems with clients who have reached a plateau, she said the first thing she wants to know is "Are they getting enough exercise and activity" She explains, "Food and the activity go hand in hand -   the combination is a critical element for success. Sometimes they are too exhausted to exercise."

The last hurdle in permanent weight loss is eating a good breakfast. Dorothy put it clearly: "The people that have breakfast keep the weight off. Breakfast sets the tone for the day. It is the most important meal of the day. You want it to be full of really great nutrients, not high in sugar or fat." One item that I had to give up was cranberry juice. I used to drink at least three glasses a day. Dorothy had to set me straight when I went for counseling due to gestational diabetes with the triplets. She told me, "Juices, although they are full of vitamins and nutrients, are full of sugar. Often times we are removing all of the fiber in the fruit. It takes a lot of pieces of fruit to make a little juice. We drink that juice down in five seconds, but if we were to sit there, it would take a good twenty minutes to eat the three or four oranges, which is probably in the amount of juice that you are drinking. Who would want to eat three or four oranges?"

The problem with drinking a glass of juice every morning with breakfast is that the high sugar content can make one crave more sugar throughout the day. Dorothy says, "When you bring that sugar into your body and ultimately into your blood system, your sugar goes up sky-high if you just have a glass of juice by itself. So your sugar spikes and then fifteen, twenty minutes later, boom, your energy plummets." Dorothy goes on to say, "Some people will just have a snack for breakfast like a juice or a bowl of grapes or something, it wakes them up and then they crash. A half an hour later they are craving something more. 'What do I want?' they ask. 'Maybe I need some caffeine. Maybe I didn't really sleep well. Why am I tired? They'll go to the vending machine and grab a candy bar.'" I loved the comparison Dorothy used: "It [snacking] just sets you up. It's like the little rat on the wheel. You just can't get off that wheel."

A healthy breakfast includes protein, especially if one eats a carbo-hydrate or sugar. Dorothy suggests, "If you have your juice (even though I'm not a big advocate of juice) and /or piece of fruit and some protein with it, your sugar will go up but it will burn off more slowly [due to protein] instead of crashing. You get that slow burn." I asked her for examples of snacks that will keep one's energy going without creating highs and lows in energy levels. "A small handful of nuts along with a pear or a nectarine are great. Another great snack is putting peanut butter on an apple or on some crackers, having some string cheese with some fruit, or having hummus with cut veggies so you always have that protein with your carbs. Maybe try some Greek yogurt with some fruit and few little nuts on top, perfect."

I was relieved that Dorothy advocates snacks in between meals. As a mom of multiples myself, I know how many times a day I'm preparing snacks. She is not a big fan of my meringue cookies, but when I try to have the type of snacks she recommends, I do notice a boost in my energy levels. As Dorothy puts it, "If you can get in those healthy snacks throughout the day, you keep your energy level steady. You also keep your metabolism burning. Keeping a little bit of fuel in there at all times keeps that engine running. You don't get the highs and lows of blood sugar." In summary, keep a journal, keep walking, snack on carbs with proteins, and drink plenty of water. Progress occurs slowly. One may not see changes right away in the mirror or in ones clothes. When their energy levels feel better, on knows they are making progress. As Dorothy puts it, "Have a little wave instead of a roller coaster of highs and lows." Riding the waves is much more fun than getting on that roller coaster. Enjoy the ride. In life with triplets, it's a journey and so why not make it pleasur-able?

Bianca gained 27 kilograms (59.4 lbs) and lost all of her baby weight in just a few months. She participated in pre-natal and post-natal physio-aqua classes and still does physio-Fit Ball classes.

She had no back pain, no pre-term labor, and no gestational diabetes prior to delivery of her three.

Bianca S., Adelaide, Australia, GGB

Our Survey's Said...

The surveys asked the moms of multiples: (1) "How much weight did you gain?;" (2) "Did you have back pain;" (3) "Did you lose all the baby weight?;" (4) "Were you able to participate in a pre or post natal exercise class?;" and (5) "How long did it take you to lose all the baby weight?" The moms I surveyed answered as follows:

1. Average amount of weight gained in moms carrying multiples

The average weight gain of the mothers of multiples in our survey was fifty-six pounds. The number of pounds gained by the mothers of multiples varied from seven to one-hundred-and-thirty-nine pounds. These figures are similar to the amount of weight gain recommended in other proven guidelines for healthy multiple pregnancies. According to Dr. Luke, the weight-gain goal of someone who is having triplets is between fifty-eight to seventy-five pounds (10). Dr. Luke's book was recommended most frequently by the moms in our study over all other books on multiples. Since the data is congruent with Dr. Luke's recommendation, it is safe to assume that these moms of multiples in our survey are an accurate sampling of all moms of multiples. In comparison, the average weight gain for singletons is between thirty-one and forty pounds (3).

Kimberly lost all but ten pounds of the eighty pounds she gained. It took her one year and she did not do any formal exercise program.

Kimberly D., Arlington, Tennessee, BBG

Jennifer lost all of her baby weight in three to four months. She said, "Taking care of three infants as a single parent was more than enough exercise. I had no prior training – never even changed a diaper prior to their birth."

Jennifer M., Waynesboro, Virginia, BBB
Total weight gain: 130 pounds

2. Incidence of back pain in moms carrying multiples during pregnancy

The percentage of moms of multiples who experienced back pain during their pregnancy was sixty-six percent on average. About six to seven out of every ten women experienced back pain during their pregnancy. This is similar to the percentage of women pregnant with singletons who experience back pain in pregnancy. Between fifty to ninety percent of women pregnant with just one baby will experience back pain at some point during their pregnancy (7,8,9,10). I was very relieved to find out that my incidence of pain would be no greater even though I would be carrying more babies.

It is not uncommon to have back pain in pregnancy. It is usually transient and does not impact the post partum recovery unless there is a pre-existing back condition. Since the actual weight gain is more on average for a triplet pregnancy than a singleton pregnancy, I would have expected the incidents of back pain to be higher. Back pain was not a factor at all when parents were asked "What is your greatest challenge?"

Kathryn lost all [of her baby weight] but twenty pounds. It took her two years. She did prenatal yoga, and postpartum she did aerobics-step aerobics. Kathryn S., Alameda, California, GGB

Kathryn delivered at thirty-six weeks. The babies went straight home, without an NICU stay. She had no gestational diabetes, pre-term labor, or back pain during her pregnancy. She was never put on bed-rest, but she was hospitalized a few days prior to delivery due to high blood pressure.

Misty gained 45 pounds during her pregnancy and lost all of her
baby weight two months after the birth of her three.
Misty W., Bedford, Texas, GGB

3. What percentage of moms lost all their baby weight?

The answer to whether or not I would lose my baby-weight based
on the experiences of other moms of multiples was, overwhelmingly, yes.
Sixty-four percent or more than half of the moms surveyed lost all of
their baby weight. These figures were encouraging for me. I would have
expected much lower numbers.

"The greatest challenge is having time to exercise while managing
the home, work and the boys."
Christy J., Augusta, Kentucky, BBB

She lost all 65 pounds a few weeks post-partum

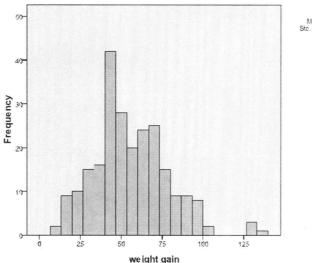

Histogram of the weight gain

4. **What is the percentage of moms of multiples who participated in group pre or post natal exercise classes?**

A great way to lose weight is to participate in group prenatal exercise classes. As stated before, the classes provide not only physical rehabilitation but a psychological and social parameter as well. The number of moms of multiples who participated in a pre or post natal exercise class was about thirty-eight percent. About one in every three moms participated in either a pre or post natal exercise group or both. Many tried pre-natal classes but had to stop because of bed-rest restrictions.

This figure is higher than I expected. Other moms of multiples can be encouraged to know that exercise classes can be worked into their schedules if they choose this method of fitness training. Exercise is a much easier pill to swallow if one has a buddy or an entire class of other moms to report to once or twice a week.

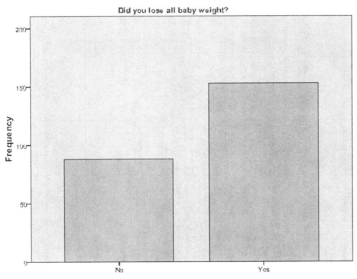

Did you lose all baby weight?

It took just a few months for Kim to lose her ninety pounds she gained during her pregnancy. She says she did "Lots of crunches post partum!"
   Kim J., Silver Spring, Maryland, BBB

5. How much time did it take moms of multiples, on average, to lose all their baby weight?

   The amount of time it took moms to lose the weight is similar to the amount recommended by many fitness instructors; to lose the weight, thirty-five weeks (35.3) or almost nine months.   In a poll of three-thousand post partum singleton moms, Elena Gorgan found that, on average, a woman needs about ten months to get her pre-baby body shape back (5). These results put my fear of never seeing my feet again, due to a multiple pregnancy to rest. Both Garner and Kidman have a reputation of taking nine months to lose their weight. "Nine months on, nine months off" is my yoga instructors' motto. This was true for the moms in our surveys as well as the moms on the tabloids. Maybe if I had known these facts I would have felt more at ease during my pregnancy.

Rene gained sixty pounds during her pregnancy and lost it within two years time. For pre-natal exercise she did walking and yoga; for post-natal, she pushed the triplet jogger and had massages if necessary. She delivered at thirty-two weeks. The babies were in the NICU one week.
   Rene I., GGG

STATISTICS
Weight Gain, Back Pain, Weight Loss, and Exercise Class Participation

1. Average Amount of Weight Gain in Moms with Multiples
The weight gain values range from 7 to 139 pounds. The average weight gain is 55.52lb with a standard deviation of 23.02lb, while the

median is 50lb. The histogram shows that the distribution is skewed to the right, with a single mode around 40-50lb. These statistics are based on 238 valid feedback responses. Note that some of the respondents seem to be either shy or unwilling to provide accurate answers. While it is very reasonable to provide a range value such as "80-85", answers such as "50+" or "15 pounds at 21 weeks" tend to pull the statistics down lower than what they should have been.

2. The Incidence of Back Pain in Moms of Multiples During Pregnancy

Based on 243 valid answers for the question concerning back pain, 160, or 65.84% (s.d. + 3.05%) answered "Yes" – as opposed to the projected 90%. We can be 95% confident that the actual overall percentage of triplet's moms who experienced back pain during pregnancy is between 59.8% and 71.8% – in other words, that will be about six or seven for every ten.

3. Percentage of Moms of Multiples Who Lost All Their Baby Weight

For the question "Did you lose all your baby weight?" Out of 241 valid responses, 153 moms (or 63.5%) answered "Yes" while the rest answered "No". The following bar chart displays the graphical comparison.

4. The Percentage of Moms of Multiples Who Participated in Group Pre or Post Natal Exercise Classes

Based on 240 valid responses regarding the question on exercise classes, 90 or 37.5% (s.d. = 3.13%) answered "Yes," which is a little over one in every three. A 95% confidence interval for the true proportion of moms who took pre or post natal exercise classes is between 31.3% and 43.7%.

5. The Amount of Time to Lose All the Baby Weight

Among those who answered "Yes" to the previous question, 150 of them provided a valid numeric answer. After converting all of the responses to numbers of weeks, it is found that the length in weeks that triplet moms take to lose all of their "baby weight" ranges from .14 week – or 1 day, (as quite a few had claimed)– to 364 weeks, or equivalently 7 years. The mean length of that process is 35.3437 weeks (s.d.=58.32 weeks). Note that the standard deviation is significantly larger here despite a large sample size. It shows that the data value has quite a big range and is dispersive.

Bibliography

1. C. Aspinwall. The busy moms' workout. Scene. D1, March 20, 2008;.

2. G. J. Bell, D. Syrotuik, T. P. Martin, R. Burnham, H. A. Quinney. Effect of concurrent strength and endurance training on skeletal muscle properties and hormone concentrations in humans. Europeon Journal of Applied Physiology. Vol. 81(5). pp 418-27, 2000.

3. A. Luis, D.W. Byrne. Optimal Maternal Weight Gain during Singelton Pregnancy. Gynecologic and Obstetric Investigation. Vol. 46(1). pp 9-16, 1998

4. E Carmeli, A Z Reznick, R Coleman, V Armeli. Muscle strength and mass of lower extremities in relation to functional abilities in elderly adults. Gerontology. Vol. 46(5): pp. 249-57, 2000.

5. M. Cronin. My new bikini body! How I did it! Star. pp. 52-9, February 1 2010.

6. E. Gorgan. March 19, 2009. Pregnant women will lose the baby weight in 10 months. Softpedia (http://news.softpedia.com/news/Pregnant - Women-Lose-the-Baby-Weight-in10-Months)

7. S. Heiwe, A Tollback, N Clyne. Twelve weeks of exercise training increases muscle function and walking capacity in elderly proteolysis patients and healthy subjects. Nephron. Vol. 88 (1). pp 48-56, 1999.

8. King-Piu Fung B, Man-Fung Kwong C, Shih-Chu Ho E. Low back pain of women during pregnancy in the mountainous district of central Taiwan. Chin Med J. Vol. 51. pp. 103-6, 1993.

9. Kristiansson P, Svardsudd K, von Schoultz B. (196) Back pain during pregnancy. A prospective study. Spine, Vol. 21. pp. 702-9, 1996.

10. B. Luke, T. Everlein. When You'r Expecting Twins, Triplets,or Quads. New York, New York. 1999.

11. Mantle MJ, Greenwood RM, Currey HLF. Backache in pregnancy. Rheumatol Rehabil, Vol. 16. pp. 95-101, 1997.

12. Nwug VCB. Pregnancy and back pain amount upper class Nigerian women. Aus J Physiother, Vol. 28. pp 8-11, 1982.

M. Tan, C. Triggs, P. Chi. Jennifer Garner - How she got her body back. People. Vol. 72(15), pp. 84-5, October 12, 2009.

D. Zinczenko. Women's Health Training Guide Lose Your Belly. Women's Helath. 2010.

Exercise equipment
Smart Bells at 800-485-0967 from Think Fit
Swiss Ball from SwissBall.com from Thera Gear
Trenna Ventions Baby Hugger's Maternity Support Brace from Cosmedical
Troo Hoops at 800-763-0909

Personal Interviews
Dorothy Bernet, MS, RD
Laurie De Jong
Deena Goodman, PT, WCS, BCIA-PMDB

CHAPTER SEVEN

. . . . .

How to Get the Help
You Will Need
Or
Batten Down the Hatches

Tracy's Story

Tracy R. is a successful OB/GYN who lives in a small town of about 30,000 people on the Gulf Coast. She and her husband tried to conceive for several years and were unsuccessful. They adopted two children, a girl and a boy, three years apart in age.

Around the age of 39, Tracy tried to conceive again with the help of ART (Assisted Reproductive Technology). After a couple rounds of IUI's (Intrauterine Insemination) they decided to try IVF (In Vitro Fertilization) using Follistim (an ovary stimulating drug). On their first (fresh) cycle, they were unsuccessful. They had only frozen embryos remaining and decided to try one last time to have a baby of their own. She told me:

"I'll be honest with you. I did IVF (In Vitro Fertilization) and it did not work in November of 2004. This was my last ditch frozen transfer. I thought, I'm going to give it up and never try again. any kind of thing." Knowing that they could get multiples, they decided to put in only two eggs. To their surprise, one egg split, giving them identical girls and one boy. Now they were in the throws of triplet pregnancy bliss.

It seemed they could swing it. They thought maybe, if they needed to, they could hire help for a short while. Her husband was an Internal medicine physician so financially they would be fine. The plan was for Tracy to go back to work when the babies were two or so. The older kids were old enough that they could help out a little. Everything was taken care of, or so it seemed.

Then, the earth moved, the wind roared, and Hurricane Katrina struck. Two weeks prior Tracy had been admitted to the hospital, when the triplets were 28-and-a-half weeks along. She said: "I went to the hospital to spend the night or so and I ended up staying there for two weeks. I was going to be discharged then suddenly my water broke, so the morning I was supposed to be discharged, so I ended up having them."

While in the hospital, the hurricane hit and the unimaginable happened. Tracy and Matt's house was destroyed. "I was a charity case because I didn't have a home to go back to." She was discharged, but had nowhere to go. The kids would stay in the NICU for now, but after that they would have to find a temporary residence. The family was able to find a rental home 45 minutes away where they would take up residence for a year. It was not exactly what they had planned. Where would they find support?

Many parents ask me, "How do you manage it, having triplets?" I guess, like many mothers of multiples, I think, "The same way you would manage it if you had the privilege of raising three beautiful babies".

Hearing Tracy's story, even I thought, "How is she going to manage that first year? She had multiple challenges: the birth and care of newborn triplets; losing her house; relocating 45 minutes away; and getting her two older kids settled in a new school district." Most people would have fallen apart with such a monstrous task.

But Tracy thrived, the triplets kept her going, and the new community's support was an unexpected surprise. Thankfully, her first year went smoothly. She told me:

"There was some press coverage because of everything that had happened. The new community rallied, I have to say. It was amazing, the support we got from them. They were wonderful. People we didn't know, in our neighborhood and the school, were helpful. It was absolutely heartwarming to think that people we didn't even know gave us furniture and clothes, and whatever we needed. They would call me and say, 'Yeah I've got this dresser,' I'd think, no, I don't need anything while I'm looking around thinking, well, you know, I just probably do. Yeah, my kids' clothes are in a box on the floor. It was a very humbling experience, I guess I would say."

When I asked Tracy how she handled comments about how she managed triplets she replied:

"When people said, I don't know how you did this or that with the triplets. Really, I think that was my saving grace. It was the fact that they were born and then lived through all of that. That was such a focus for me to keep going and for them to be healthy. During the whole first year, that's all we worried about, the kids and feeding the babies. It made everything else really trivial, at least for me. Like whatever, you know? This house, it's 'stuff'. You can replace it; but everybody is fine. We have three healthy babies. You know, the whole reality of the fact that we could have lost one. We didn't have any of that."

Another miracle occurred in that year while they were rebuilding their house. Tracy got pregnant and conceived a beautiful baby girl. As far as her plans to go back to work are concerned; they are on hold for now. She says that maybe when they all start school. For now, she's just enjoying them.

• • •

"Accept help from whoever offers it. Don't be too proud or too embarrassed to have someone do your laundry, clean your dishes or vacuum your rugs."
Christine C., Kensington, Connecticut, GGB

"The biggest challenge is keeping up with all of the household duties in addition to taking care of the babies. Be organized, have a plan, get help with household chores and meals if possible."
Michelle R., Springfield, Missouri, BBG

"GET HELP and get a schedule!"
Julie B, Colorado

"Be flexible, accept help, and sacrifice privacy temporarily to accept help." Terry P., Anacortes, Washington, BBG

Help: How Much is Enough?

One compelling reason to write this book was to answer questions that I couldn't find in the literature I examined. Nowhere is there a formula for how much help you will need to survive the demands of three or more babies. There's a recommendation for how much weight to gain in a multiple pregnancy, how many diapers you'll need to buy, or what baby accessories are essential for multiples; But no one says, that from day one you will need extra help; lots of extra help. How much you can afford will determine how much you will get to some degree. However, many parents I talked to made it work by accepting help in places they never thought existed.

Help can take many shapes and sizes. You can hire help. Family and friends can help. Depending on where you live, you can get assistance in the community from church or other social organizations. People have different attitudes and responses about receiving help. Some of us are happy to receive help. When help is given, we respond graciously, making the giver happy to continue giving. One mom of multiples said: "When someone offers you help, take it. Don't be proud. It's humbling to have to need help, but face the facts, you do." Many of us have a hard time receiving help from the outside. We prefer to be as independent as possible, but we will accept help in certain circumstances. Karin, a mother of multiples from New Jersey, said: "I wish I would have accepted more assistance. If I had it to do over again, I would have hired more help." Then, there are some of us who "tough-it-out," doing fine on our own..

"How much help did you need?" I asked on the web questionnaire and in most interviews. Many interviewees say they wish they had accepted help more often. In fact, one woman clearly said, "If I had it to do all over again, I would have taken out a home loan, just to get more help." This desire for more help is a common thread in the fabric of multiple parenting. I never did find a succinct answer to how much help is enough, but I did find that others were clever and creative in ways that surprised even themselves. Just try to leave the door open for making room in your house for unexpected visitors and learn to say no when you've had enough.

Post a note on your family web-site or on the front of your door, requesting visitors to come only if they are well. Spell-out what boundaries are important to you and your family. Define what a "sick" visitor is and it won't be as hard to ask them to leave.
Anonymous

When Help is Not Helpful

When it comes to volunteers coming into your house to help, be it family or otherwise, it is important to protect the kids at all costs. It's easy to tell a nanny whom you are paying what to do, such as, "Go home, you're sick." But, most find it exponentially more difficult to set boundaries with their own family. I remember one woman of GBG (girl-boy-girl) triplets told me how her favorite aunt came from out of state to visit and stay with them to help out for a week. She had a runny nose, and thought it was her "allergies." The babies were home from the NICU just shy of four weeks. They were all living in a small, two – bedroom apartment and, low and behold, the Mom and one of the girls both ended up in the hospital with their aunt's "allergy." The mom said she had hesitated about being cautious because the NICU nurses told her that once the babies left the NICU to treat them just like regular babies. No matter what anyone says, preemies are more susceptible to illness.

From Fall to Spring it is the "RSV time of year" (respiratory syncytial virus). Helen R., a mom of BBB triplets from Missouri, actually posted visitor guideline on their family's web site:

Family and Friends,

We're really looking forward to introducing (and showing off) our babies to all of you! However, because they are preemies we need to be extra careful about germs. Preemies are especially at risk for RSV which is a very serious illness in babies, often times resulting in hospitalization. As a result of this risk, we will be exceedingly careful during RSV season (fall to spring) and appreciate your willingness to keep our babies safe and healthy!

1. *Please call or e-mail us prior to visiting - we will be trying to keep a per day visitor limit.*
2. *You, any members of your family, and anyone you work closely with or spend a lot of time with, MUST not be sick or have been sick in the last 5 days! "Sick" includes:*

Cough	*Fever*
Sore Throat	*Intestinal Flu*
Sneezing/Runny Nose	*Diarrhea*

3. *Upon entering our home, you will immediately wash and sanitize your hands.*
4. *If you touch your face or hair, please re-sanitize your hands.*
5. *At this time, we ask that you please refrain from kissing the babies and putting your fingers on or in their mouths.*

Thanks again for your understanding!

Sometimes you need to be a little more direct. Another family actually posted a sign on their door. The Mom said that her husband composed it because it was mostly his family that was imposing, and she didn't want direction coming from her. It went something like this: "Thank you for visiting, we are napping from *this time* to *this time*, if you are visiting during this time, please come again."

"We had help in and out for awhile but we wanted to do it on our own from the beginning! They were mostly Starbucks delivery, dinner makers, and drivers for our older daughter."
Ami C., 3 year old BBG Triplets and 7 year old daughter
Avon, Ohio

Family Help

There are many ways you can seek and receive help. Paid help is one option. Another possibility is to accept donated time, money, and resources. Friends and family often offer this kind of assistance. Amy, a triplet mom from Ohio, said she could not afford any part-time or full-time paid help. In response, her grandmother offered to hire a nanny for a few hours a day for the first three months. Amy accepted. She found someone to come in during "fussy time", the 4-7 p.m. hour (otherwise known as the witching hour). This break helped tremendously. As we all know, this is the most difficult time of the day.

"My son's whole sixth grade class pitched in and sent home second hand stuff, cribs, etc."
   Kris D., Jewett City, Connecticut
   BBG and an older son in grade school

Community Help

In one interview, Heidi T, a mother of BBG triplets, explained how not only meals but supplies were donated. She described a community service that was done for her family by their church: a diaper drive. I had heard of a blood drive before, but never a diaper drive. "What's that?" I inquired. "The church put an ad in their weekly bulletin and asked for the members to bring in diapers for us every week." She went on: "Every couple of weeks or so they would call us to see what size diapers the kids were in." She had my attention: "The kids are almost two now, and we haven't had to buy a single diaper!" I was so touched. What an amazing display of compassion. In her case, she said they were new to the community and many of the donations came from perfect strangers.

One excellent piece of advice I've had on help is getting a handicap placard. I remember someone suggesting this early on, when our kids were only a few months old. But the thought of *me* getting a handicap placard seemed absurd. As a physical therapist, I had worked with people with significant physical challenges, such as sip and puff wheelchairs. They deserve placards, not me; but this time I listened to this woman's advice. Jen K. from California said: "It just wasn't safe to unload the babies into the triplet stroller situated behind the van, while I went back into the van, one at a time, to get more kids out. Someone could walk away with one of the kids or hit the stroller because it hung out so far in the parking lot." Safety of the children is top priority. What pediatrician wouldn't sign off on that? It's easy to just download an application from the DMV website. It costs five dollars and a call to the pediatricians' office.

"Trial and error is the best way to learn not to be afraid to fail, you can learn something from every new situation. Even though something may seem impossible, give it a try. Look at each new experience as a mini victory. Also, be sure to find a support group for parents with multiples so you can have people who have been there to offer advice, support and provide humor."
Shelli K., Oswego, Illinois, BBG

Support from Other Mothers of Multiples

I hear it all the time: pair up and find someone to talk to whenever you are trying to get through something difficult. I just never thought parenting would be something I was "going through." I thought it would be a lifelong pleasure-cruise type of journey, like the "Love Boat," rather then a ship-wreck on the rocky seas of life. It is a unique challenge unparalleled by our singleton parent friends and their families. Few of us have parents who also had twins or triplets. Maybe there is some distant cousin in Arkansas, who lived in a shoe and beat her children because she had so many she didn't know what to do! Our parenting compass deviates slightly from those of our family members. The advice we get from loved ones sometimes does not apply because they are used to how it was when they raised their kids, one at a time. Although professionals

are well meaning, I feel more comfortable taking the advice of a psychologist or pediatrician when I know they have had experience with
multiples in some way.

One thing is certain, having someone to talk to, who has been where
you are going or is on the same path you are, makes the journey much
more pleasant. I was recently was invited to join a group of triplet Moms
for dinner. They have been getting together once a month for dinner
since their triplets were born. A couple even knew each other when they
were pregnant with their triplets. Their kids range from 17 months to
two years. Two of them have GGB and one had BBG triplets, like I have.
One of them came to dinner, even though it was her triplet's second
birthday that day. Now that's dedication! Obviously there must be
something here for them. Is it safety in numbers? Maybe it's just that
we'd been e-mailing back and forth for the past month, and they were
just tired of my endless e-mails? Maybe, but probably more importantly,
they find comfort in having each other to talk to and share their evening
and lives. It's the treasured opportunity to relate to someone with similar
issues, someone who can answer those burning questions that burden
the mother of multiples.

Looking at them you couldn't guess their common denominator.
They are all in excellent physical condition. No belly battle scars or
sagging mid sections among them. They are attractive, energetic, and
full of life – none of them look haggard or overtired. All are balancing
part or full time jobs, along with the 24-7 job of being a parent of multiples. One works in the entertainment industry, one is an attorney, and
the other a realtor. They all are burdened with a fair dose of "Mommy
guilt" – common to all Moms who work (or stay at home) – finding a
way to spend enough time with each child individually and still have
space for them to breathe. They ask each other such questions as: How
do you get the kids to eat healthy food when you're not there for a few
hours during the day? At what age do you start brushing their teeth?
Where can you find both kid-friendly and reasonably priced meals in
town? What activities can you do on the weekends for the whole family

where the kids can run around and burn off energy and yet not get snatched or run over? Where are the kid-friendly museums or concerts in the park?

This first meeting was a busy evening. We chatted non-stop for over two hours. When we were done, they all looked at me and said: "We didn't answer any your interview questions!" What they didn't realize is that they gave me more then I needed for a month's worth of writing by asking each other questions ranging from when to fire the night-nanny to how soon to expect your kids to walk? One shared a story of her husband who couldn't follow through with his vasectomy, even after scheduling himself for surgery three times, while another Mom told about making sure she had her tubes tied the same day she delivered her triplets. They were all different. Yet they all had one thing in common: they are all survivors of the triplet Mom journey in LA.

Another Mother of triplets wrote a story in Supertwins about how her e-mail, cyber mom friends (also mothers of Higher-Order Multiples) sent her daughter a special box of cheer when she was going through a rough time and needed bilateral lung transplant surgery. The box of cheer went around the world to all the cyber moms and their kids to gather well wishes. It ook three years to get to her, but when it did she opened up a box with a stuffed bear, signed by all the kids, a story-telling notebook about every country the bear had been in, and various get well add-ons, like a necklace, a bracelet, angel wings, and good luck beach glass. At the end of the article the Mom wrote: "It's hard to put into words how touched I was at the magnitude of this generous gift that was given to my daughter. We feel the embrace of support around us every hour of every day. Knowing that so many people care so much about our daughter gives us such strength and peace of mind." This story was a true testament to how much stronger mothers are when they come together for support.

"My advice to new parents of multiples is to find help first of all if you feel depressed, don't be ashamed."
   Kim L., Wethersfield, Connecticut, BBG

"When the babies first came we had no idea that we'd never have a minute to eat supper and take a shower. My advice to other moms of multiples is to accept the help and get organized."
   Jodi C., Lowelville, Ohio, GGB

"Post-partum depression hits at 10 weeks."
   Shannon D., Riverside , BBG Triplets

What the Experts Say
Warning Signs: When You Need More Support
Rita Suri, MD Associate Professor of Psychiatry at UCLA Semel Institute of Neuro science and Human Behavior

When a mother's emotional well-being is at stake, there should be no limit to providing her with the optimal amount of support she may need, be it financial, emotional, or professional; but, we all know we don't live in a perfect world. With health care costs at a premium, mental health services are not always reimbursed appropriately. Mothers of multiples have the potential for all of the same psychological stresses that mothers of singletons have as well as other potential problems: feelings of guilt; inadequate time for three or more children all at the same time; social isolation; marital difficulties; and domestic overload. These normal stresses often are exacerbated by intrusive questions from strangers about implying that triplets are abnormal and/or questioning as to what medical intervention was used to produce the triplets.

One thing to be careful of is Post Partum Depression. In 2003 a study of 587 Mothers of Supertwins (MOST) – mothers of higher-order-multiples – 29 percent had depression after the birth of their multiples

(7). According to a study of 758 mothers of twins and higher-order multiples done by the National Organization of Mothers of Twins Clubs Inc. (NOMOTC), mothers of multiple birth children are more at risk for this illness because of the already tremendous physical, financial, and psychological stressors they face (7). In the NOMOTC study, the rate of Postpartum Depression was found to be 37 percent. Primarily moms of twins were polled in the study (95% compared to 5 percent triplet and other parents). There are some common threads that mothers of higher order multiples may find interwoven with their friends who are parents of twins. Singleton studies on Postpartum Depression (PPD) have generally shown the prevalence to be between ten and twenty-five percent in the first postpartum year, depending on the risk factors (4). Mothers who are at high risk for PPD include those with poor social support, those caring for multiple other small children in the house (prior to the birth of the new baby), a history of previous depression or family history of depression or if the mother has a history of post partum depression, with previous pregnancies.

Of those respondents in the NOMOTC study experiencing depression postpartum, 25% did seek professional help. Other problems such as marital tension (35%) and feelings of isolation, guilt, or inadequacy (43%), were also reported up to one year after birth. A large majority of mothers (70%) reported that joining a multiples club/support group was instrumental in helping maintain good mental health. It is true that there is safety in numbers.

Postpartum Depression is clinically defined as a "major depressive episode that occurs in the first four weeks after delivery" (Diagnostic and Statistical Manual of Mental Disorders-IV or DSM-IV). Although the DSM says patients are most susceptible in the first month, clinically, the experts say it can happen any time in the first year. I had a personal interview with Dr. Rita Suri, a professor at the UCLA Semel Institute of Neuroscience and Human Behavior whose research interests focus on mood disorders during pregnancy and the postpartum period. She said, "The most vulnerable period is between three weeks and six months after delivery." The three categories of Postpartum Depression Disorders are postpartum "blues", postpartum major depression, and postpartum psychosis. The most common syndrome is "baby blues", with 50-85% prevalence. Symptoms include fatigue, difficulty concentrating, irritability, mood swings, and fluctuations in appetite. In the NOMOTC survey almost half of the moms (47%) confirmed experiencing "baby blues." It usually lasts less than two weeks. However, if a mother experiences the "blues" for longer, she may need further evaluation and medication to help her through the depression. Postpartum Psychosis, thankfully, only occurs in 0.1 percent of all postpartum women, and is thought to be a variant of bipolar disorder. Patients with this diagnosis need aggressive, in-patient treatment because of the risk of suicide and/or infanticide.

For patients who surpass the "baby blues" phase into major depression, a psychiatrist will often recommend an anti-depressant medication (most typically an SSRI or selective serotonin reuptake inhibitor) or psychotherapy, or a combination of both. The SSRI drugs are safe for women who are nursing babies of any age. Dr. Suri has seen these drugs used even in the NICU on mothers with premature babies. "The perinatalogists and I agree that treatment won't stop just because a mother is nursing. We will monitor the babies and look for changes in sleep patterns, colic, or growth issues. But developing babies are always changing, having growth spurts that upset sleeping patterns or eating issues that interfere with growth, so you can't blame it on the medication." For most people this type of medication is very helpful and has minimal side effects.

• • •

Signs and Symptoms of Post Partum Depression

Changes in appetite and sleep patterns (up or down)
Lack of interest in all activities
Fatigue
Feelings of anger, worthlessness, hopelessness
Forgetfulness
Poor personal hygiene
Excessive anxiety
Isolating behaviors
Fear of being alone with or harming the babies or oneself
Ruminations of persistent negative thoughts,
i.e. "Will the baby stop breathing at night"

Dr. Suri has just completed a five year NIH study grant from three clinical sites on the risk factors of post partum depression. She recalled one mother of twins in the study who showed signs early on in the pregnancy and sought treatment. When it came time for her to go on bed rest, she had already established a relationship with a therapist and was able to have phone therapy. She obviously couldn't leave her house to get to the clinic. Dr. Sure was surprised how well this mom coped considering her risk factors. She mentioned that being an older mom may have had something to do with it. She had waited longer to have children and had planned for it. She knew that since she was having twins that more help around the house would be needed so she tried to set that in place before the babies were even born. "Many times," Dr Suri said, "it's just a matter of the Moms changing their expectations. It's important not to feel like you have to be the perfect Mom."

Try and take some time for yourself and when you are feeling over-
whelmed pick up the phone and call a family member or a friend to come
and help. Almost 100% of the time people are willing to help if we just let
them know.

Crystal H., Noble, BBG

Stick Together

If we stick together we cannot be broken. There is an old African riddle that asks: "Which is better to have one big stick or many small sticks?" The answer: Many small sticks. Why? They can be bound together and made exponentially stronger. Once bound, they cannot be broken even if you try to wrap them over your knee to break them. With only 6000 triplet births per year in the US, our numbers are small so it may be difficult to find another triplet mom to connect with. However do try to go out and find a play group or a Mom's group or even just another mother of multiples to grab a cup of coffee with and start networking. Stick together.

In other words, receive all the help you can get: from placards, to nannies, to church friends, to aunts, to other mothers of multiples, and to signs on your door. At another time in your life, having graciously received, you will know how to graciously give to others.

Our Surveys Said...

More than three-quarters (81.1%) of families of multiples had help from their families. The amount of time help came varied tremendously. Their replies varied from two days of help to ten years of help from family members. The average amount of time family came to help out was six-and-a-half months. Whether or not families of multiples received help from their family members did not depend on what part of the country they lived in or whether they were domestic or foreign. Family help was a universal theme. Paid help was not as universal.

Although parents commented that they wished they had more help or hired more help, most of them did not enlist paid, outside help. An overwhelming 73 % said "No" they did not hire help during the day, and 84 % did not hire help at night.   This question may have been a more delicate subject than other ones on the questionnaire because fewer parents answered this question than almost any other one on the questionnaire (177 compared to 241).

The remaining 27 % who did hire outside help had that help from as little as one day to as long as ninety-six months or eight years. The amount of time people hired help during the day came on average was nine-and-a-half months. The length of time parents of multiples hired night help, ranged from one week to eight years for three months on average. Those who hired night help made up only 16 %.

Average amount of help from family during the day for parents of multiples

Among 241 valid responses, 48 of them (or 19.9%) stated clearly "no", while the other 193 listed answers from (simply) "yes" (and did not provide a length), to "random", "whenever asked" and the like. These responses are all considered "yes" to the question "Did you get help from family?" Therefore, it is not surprising to see a large proportion of triplet parents who used or are still using help from their family.

The responses vary in terms of frequency and duration. Some families provided a frequency rather than duration, others did not even bother to leave any length after they confirmed on using family help). Based on 144 valid responses ranging from 2 days to 10 years (some are still ongoing), the average length of family help is 6.5 months with a standard deviation of 2.88 months. The distribution is strongly right-skewed, as shown in the next histogram.

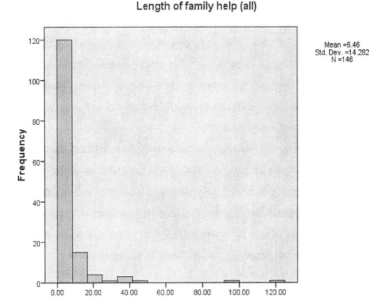

The median length is 2.9 months. First and third quartiles are .9 and 6 months, respectively. This means that about a quarter of the surveyed parents enlisted family help for less than a month while roughly another quarter uses help from the family for more than half a year.

Average amount of paid help during the day for families of multiples

Out of 241 valid responses to the question regarding hired day help, 177 (or 73.4%) answered "no" while 64 (or 26.6%) answered "yes"

Not all parents who enlisted day help provided the duration. Some wrote frequencies such as "twice a week", but forgot to mention how long. Among the remaining 47 valid responses, the mean and standard deviation are found to be 18.9 months and 20.9 months, respectively. The day help duration ranges from 1 month to 96 month (8 years) with a median of 9.5 months. (Therefore, the distribution is heavily skewed to the right.) Some of the day help is still ongoing.

Among 240 valid responses to the question regarding hired night help, 38 answered "yes" and 202 answered "no". The corresponding proportions are 15.8% and 84.2%, respectively.

Average amount of paid help at night for families of multiples

From 30 people who provided a valid numeric response for the duration of the night help, the mean and standard deviation can be found to be 8.4 months and 17.3 months, respectively. The times vary from .23 months (1 week) to 96 months (8 years) (with a median of 3 months), and just as in duration for day help, some of which is still ongoing.

Summary of average amount of hired help day and night for families of multiples

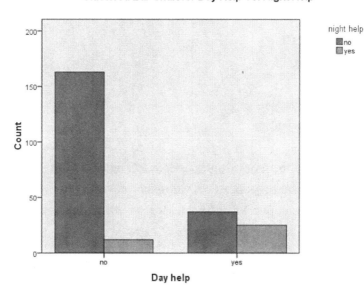

Clustered Bar Chart for Day Help Vs. Night Help

International Multiple Birth Organizations
(A list of support organizations from the National Organization of
Mother's of Twins Club, Inc., www.nomotc.org)

Association of Finnish Triplet Families (Finland): There are stories
and photos of triplets, an English section and lots of international
links.
Australian Multiple Birth Association (AMBA): AMBA is a nonprofit
organization whose goals are to increase awareness of the special needs
of multiple birth families, and to improve the resources available to
them.

COMBO: Council of Multiple Birth Organizations, a working group
of the International Society for Twin Studies. Promotes sharing of
ideas and resources among multiple birth organizations throughout
the world.

Doppelt & Dreifac, Mehrlingselterninitiative Giessen e.v. (Germany)
(Site is in German)

European Twins (Italy)
(Site is in Italian)

IKRESEK (Hungary)
(Site is in Hungarian)

Irish Multiple Births Associations (Ireland): The Irish Multiple Births
Association is a young Association, whose objectives are to improve
current services and to act as advocates for parents and their families
of twins, triplets and higher multiples.

International Society for Twin Studies: ISTS is an international,
nonpolitical, nonprofit, multidisciplinary scientific organization. Its

purpose is to further research and public education in all fields related to twins and twin studies, for the mutual benefit of twins and their families and of scientific research in general.

International Twins Association, Inc.: ITA is a nonprofit organization promoting the spiritual, intellectual and social welfare of twins throughout the world. ITA has been meeting every Labor Day weekend since 1934.

Jumeaux et plus, l'Association Fédération (France)
(Site is in French)

Multifamilias (Argentina) Multifamilias is the first support foundation for multiple birth parents in Argentina. Multifamilias publishes a maganize in spanish annually. (Site is in Spanish)

Multiple Births Canada/Naissances Multiples Canada (MBC): Multiple Births Canada (MBC) is a national non-profit organization serving the needs of multiple birth families. MBC's mission is to improve the quality of life for multiple birth individuals and their families across Canada. MBC provides support, education, research, and advocacy to individuals, families, and organizations with a personal or professional interest in multiple birth issues.

Multiplos (Brazil)
(Site is in Portuguese)

New Zealand Multiple Births Association (New Zealand)

PADRES MÚLTIPLES (Argentena): "PADRES MÚLTIPLES" is a non profit Organization which main goals are: share scientific information as well as everyday experiences, give emotional support in difficult times and help parents of multiples in need. "PADRES MÚLTIPLES" is an Argentinean organization but we have members from all over the world, including US citizens. Our web page is in Spanish though we have several English speaking members to help.

Svenska Trillingföreningen (Sweden)
(Site is in Swedish)

TAMBA (Twins and Multiples Births Association) (England): TAMBA is a registered charity for all parents with twins, triplets, quads, quints, sextuplets or more! It supports families with twins or more, individually, through local twins clubs, and specialist support groups, and promotes public and professional awareness of their needs.

Other Support Organizations
M.O.S.T. (Mothers of Supertwins): A national, nonprofit network providing information, resources, empathy, and support to families with triplets and more.

Multiplicity: The Special Challenges of Parenting Twins & More - Loss, Prematurity and Special Needs. Lists organizations, print & website resources that may be helpful for parents facing the challenges of raising multiples, working through loss of one or more multiples, or raising one or more premature or special needs child(ren).

Triplet Connection: Triplet Connection, a non-profit, tax exempt organization, is a "Network of Caring and Sharing" for multiple-birth families. It provides vital information to families who are expecting triplets, quadruplets, quintuplets or more, as well as encouragement, resources, and networking opportunities for families who are parents of higher order multiples.

Twins Days in Twinsburg, Ohio: Each year during the first full weekend in August, a festival is held in Twinsburg, Ohio (about 30 miles south of Cleveland). It's reported to be the largest annual gathering of twins in the world.

Bibliography

1. VK Burt, R Suri, L Altshuler, Z Stowe, VC Hendrick. The Use of Psychotropic Medications During Breast-Feeding. American Journal of Psychiatry, 2001.

2. LS Cohen, R Nonacs, AC Viguera, AM Reminick, LL. Antidepressant Treatment and Relapse of Depression During Pregnancy. The Journal of the American Medical Association, 2006.

3. LS Cohen, LL Altshuler, BL Harlow, R Nonacs, DJ. Relapse of Major Depression During Pregnancy in Women Who Maintain or Discontinue Antidepressant. Obstetrical & Gynecological Survey, 2006.

4. Gale and Harlow. Literature Review. Journal of Psychosomatic Obstetrics and Gynecology, 2003 (a review of clinical and epidemiologic factors affecting postpartum mood disorders).

5. M Garel, B Blondel. Assessment at 1 Year of the Psychological Consequences of Having Triplets. Human Reproduction vol. 7, no 5. pp 7290732, 1992.

6. MJ Gitlin, R Suri. Management of Side Effects of SSRIs and Newer Antidepressants. Practical Management of the Side Effects of Psychotropic ..., 1999.

7. S Griffith. Postpartum Depression in Mothers of Multiples COMBO Editor, National Organization of Mothers of Twins Clubs, Inc. Web

publication '07. Abstracts for the ISTS Mid-Congress Conference Los Angeles, June 29, 2005.

8. V Hendrick, LL Altshuler, R Suri. <u>Hormonal changes in the postpartum and implications for postpartum depression</u>. Psychosomatics, 1998 - womensmentalhealth.org.

9. V Hendrick, LM Smith, R Suri, S Hwang, D Haynes, L. <u>Birth outcomes after prenatal exposure to antidepressant medication.</u> American Journal of Obstetrics & Gynecology, 2003.

10. V Hendrick, ZN Stowe, LL Altshuler, J Mintz, S. <u>Fluoxetine and norfluoxetine concentrations in nursing infants and breast milk</u>. Biological Psychiatry, 2001.

11. R Suri, L Altshuler, G Hellemann, VK Burt, <u>Effects of Antenatal Depression and Antidepressant Treatment on Gestational Age at Birth and Risk</u>. American Journal of Psychiatry, 2007.

12. R Suri, ZN Stowe, V Hendrick, A Hostetter. <u>Estimates of nursing infant daily dose of fluoxetine through breast milk</u>. Biological Psychiatry, 2002.

13. Verkerk, Gerda, et. Al. <u>Prediction of depression in the postpartum period: A longitudinal follow-up study in high-risk and low-risk women.</u> Journal of Affective Disorders, Vol. 77 (2). pp. 159-166, 2003.

14. Walsh, S. <u>Annie's Fairy Bear.</u> Supertwins. Vol18, No 1. pp 8-10, 2008.

Personal Interviews
Tracey Roth
Rita Suri, MD

CHAPTER EIGHT

. . . . . .

*School Days – Divide & Conquer
or Stick Together
Or
Cartography of School Age
Multiples*

Marci's Story

Marci M. is a medical billing manager in Missouri. She runs her practice out of her home. She has two sets of twins (BG/GG) and anolder singleton daughter. She is a single parent. All of her kids go to public school.

I asked Marci to help answer some school age questions and she was happy to oblige. First I asked the obvious question, "Did you separate your twins into different classes and why?"

She quite clearly stated, "We wanted them separate from the get go. When they started school we made sure they were in separate classes." She continued, "We wanted them to have their own identities, their own set of friends, and their own personalities. We've never really even dressed them the same."

Her oldest is now seventeen years old. The older twins are in middle school, age twelve (GG), and grammar school, age eight (BG). All five have gone through public school in separate classes. I wanted to know what it's like now that they are older.

She went on, "It's to the point where our middle school kids do sets of classes in their separate groups. One is in the safari group, the other in the adventure core, with separate teachers. They don't have the same anything-at-all. It's totally separate. And, it's their choice. They get along better that way."

Marci explained that by having separate classes they have a unique experiences, are being able to make their very own friends and do their own activities.

She explained, "They feel like they have to share so much that they don't want to share any more than they have to."

Aside from classroom separation, the logistics of how to manage all five at once was getting the better of my curiosity. "How do you manage having kids at different ages? Isn't it actually more work when they are spread out?" I asked.

She said, "The strengths of one compliment the others' weaknesses. Some of them are good with the littler kids and some of them are good

She said, "The strengths of one compliment the others' weaknesses. Some of them are good with the littler kids and some of them are good in the kitchen."

Thinking about how my boys love to wrestle and think our new baby is really a doll of sorts. I asked Marci what her tricks were to getting them to behave "nicely" to one another.

She said, "Right now one of the middle schoolers is really good with the little ones. She tutors them for 'pocket money.' She helps them with their school. She has a bossy personality. So, she does homework with them, when they need reading done, she sits with them."

I told her about our "chore chart" for our five-year-olds at home. We have a list of a few items we ask them to do daily, such as make their bed. If they comply they earn a dime for each item. I wanted to know if she did something similar.

She agreed chores were important. Giving them a sense of responsibility, ownership, and discipline is necessary. Without structure, the home would be chaos.

"They make their own lunch. Even the little ones; they are eight right now, they do their own laundry, make their own beds, put their clothes away. One of them makes dinner." She continued with a funny comment about their dinner time routine. "My little one just learned to make grilled cheese sandwiches; she's constantly trying to get everyone to eat them."

I asked her why she felt they were so good at doing so much on their own and she replied, "They are very independent and they are great that way because they only have one parent and they have to take care of themselves."

I asked about other twins in Marci's town and how the parents treated them. In particular I wanted to know if they were as independent and self motivated as Marci's. To this question she replied "There is a set of twins in my daughters' class; they are in seventh grade. They wear the same clothes, and ride the same kind of bikes. It's so weird to see that. They can't be without the other one."

I was curious to know if the school had ever made special allowances for either set of twins. She said that they did. "If I ask for something they do it. I did ask them to run a group therapy for one of my girls because she has a hard time making friends. It was recommended by the school's therapist."

She went on to tell the story of her daughters' difficult first year in kindergarten due to her ADHD and high functioning autism. "She was not medicated and she had a really difficult time. She would destroy things. It was just awful. We couldn't control her. So they put her on medication and she got much better."

Since she lived in a small community where everybody knew each other, it made it difficult for her daughter the following year in first grade. She went on, "Kids were scared to be friends with her, scared to open up with her and they didn't like her very much."

"So, her therapist (the one the school provides) that sees her once a week, suggested that we have them start a group at school so they can kind of get together on a different level."

I thought that an organized group was a clever way to bridge the gap and make new acquaintances, but I wondered if it would work. Kids can be mean and change takes time.

Luckily for Marci's daughter school started to become more manageable. Marci explained.

"So, at lunch, they get together and the school counselor is there to help them and see that they get together on a different level. It took awhile to get started but the school was all for it. And, once a week they have a little lunch group. She's making friends now."

Marci had to request that the school make some changes to circumvent a difficult situation, but in the end it worked out for the best.

• • •

"We initially separated the kids by choice. After two years we put them in the same class. It has not been an issue with the children or teachers and makes life somewhat easier. It has been the same situation with sports although they are beginning to choose their own interests and are often doing their own thing. The great thing is to see them cheer each other on. I love it!"

Brenda S., Jonesville, Virginia. GGB

"We tried six weeks of public school then moved to private. In the private school they had one kindergarten, so they were kept together. We had no issues at the private school. We decided to home school for first grade. In Pennsylvania you don't have to register kids in school until they are eight years old."

Angela P., Lake Ariel, Pennsylvania, 21 y/o boy, 18 y/o girl
6 y/o triplets (BBG), 5 y/o singleton

"The girls were placed on the boy's soccer teams. They were not separated in school classes; they are in the top ten percent in high school for academics."

Patti M., St. John, Indiana, GGB

"My kids attend a small school with only one class per grade. The boys have historically been on the same soccer team but as they get older, they no longer play all the same sports."

Erin W., West Sacramento, California, BBG

Kindergarten Days

For us, separating the kids in school seemed necessary and inevitable at some point in time. Yet, when I received the kids' letters just before kindergarten from their different teachers, I suddenly felt uneasy about their first separation. In a knee-jerk reaction, I phoned the principal. Surely she had nothing better to do than to calm me down, after all she did have only three days left before school started. To my delight she called me back. We discussed the, "unwritten district-wide school twin policy" which separates all twins, unless otherwise requested, prior to the start of the school year. I can't say I didn't know how the school handled twins. I had experience in the past with my senior high school child in the same school district. He had had a set of triplets in his grade who had been separated all through grade school. They had been separated all through grade school, middle and high school.

This time, I played dumb for a little while to see if the conversation could be spun to include understanding of multiples. "I just want to know if you are flexible," I inquired. "I'm not trying to make waves. But if this all goes 'South,' and my kids miss each other terribly, can we revisit this issue about separate classes? I know it's unusual. I'm really not concerned about them separating from me, but it's the separation from each other that worries me." Then I poured it on a bit thicker: "They shared the same womb, and you neither you nor I can know what that's like. Plus, in two years of preschool, my kids were never apart from each other." She thought for a minute, and reiterated the "school policy." Then, she threw me a curve. "We put these classes together months ago. Why didn't you let us know sooner that this was what you wanted?" I couldn't give her a good answer. I truly didn't know what I wanted. I just knew that my inner conflict, between what I wanted originally, and what was going to happen in a few days, seemed too scary to survive.

I also knew that I was losing the battle. "But, but, I just got these letters in the mail. I didn't know it was the policy. I was in the same school district for preschool, and nobody separated them then." We discussed things further. She recited what many educators feel is the gospel truth. Children can't "individuate" unless they are separated. After we had heard each other's side, all of the cards were on the table. I had said my piece; the principal knew where I stood. We agreed to try it 'as is' with the kids in separate classes and talk again in a couple weeks. Thankfully, and to my husband's prediction and delight, that conversation never happened. Our three would make it work one way or another.

I knew one other mother whose twin boys had been separated in preschool. Their sister, Becca, was in Alex's kindergarten class. On the first day of school in September, Becca's Mom relayed a 'first day of preschool' story of her now seven-year-old, twin boys. She said, "We waited until the day before school started to tell them they would be separated. We knew they would be unhappy, and we didn't want them to worry about it for days on end. When we told our first boy, he said, 'I don't want to talk about it,' and walked away. When we told our second boy, he just went up to his room and started crying." Then she went on to tell me what happened that night after she had tucked them into their beds; "When I went to check on them, one of the boys had gotten out of his bed and climbed into bed with the other one. They snuggled together for weeks, those first few weeks of school."

I thought this was such a great story that I told it to my kids over dinner that night. After I relayed Becca's Mom's story, my three suddenly stopped eating and ran upstairs. Before I could prevent them from their plan, they had dismantled all of their beds and plopped them on the floor next to each other, side by side, touching. Samy, my little girl, said, "They can separate us in school, but we're not going to sleep separately!" Jack and Alex agreed. Jack said, "It's just like when we were in your tummy, Mom. 'Pea Pod babies.' Remember?"

Looking back on the complete blur of those first few weeks, I realize now that it could have been a positive or negative experience either way; together or separate. What mattered was that I had to keep an open mind and heart, listen to what the kids' responses were, and wait and hope for the best outcome. I knew if I had a preconceived set of ideas one way or another, it might promote a disaster. As it turned out, they all blossomed in their various classrooms. They missed each other during class time, but they saw each other at lunch and recess. They made separate friends. The closeness they missed in class, they made up for at home, especially at night.

"We have a really good public school. When they went into kindergarten and first grade they started a pilot program. It's called a looping program. In the program, they could stay with the same class and same teacher.

Because I stayed home with them for the first four years, I thought it'd be good for them to stay together in this program. They did it for the first two years.

They are in fifth grade now. Starting in second grade they all went on their own. They adapted just fine but it was rough doing homework. Homework with three different kids and three different teachers means two to three different sets of homework. Now I have them in the same grouping so at least all of the homework is the same and it's working out better.

I started the Triplets Network in Ocean County and I keep in touch with the moms. The funny part is, some will tell you they're placed all together and some will tell you they're all separate. Some just swear by them being separate; it's sort of like half and half."

Jane M., Manahawkin, New Jersey, GGB

"My three are three years old and will be entering pre-school in September. The school wants to separate them, but I don't."

Erin P., East Bridgewater, Massachusetts, BBG

What the Expert's Say

Nancy Segal, a developmental psychologist specializing in twin research, surveyed sixty-three parents from the Minneapolis-Saint Paul area. She found that nearly half of the mothers whose twins' schools had a mandatory separation policy did not endorse it (1 – Segal & Russell, 1992). She feels "The current consensus (among both parents and investigators) is that each pair should be handled on a case-by-case basis, but apparent lack of flexibility in many schools does not allow this" (2).

According to "Twinslaw.com" as of November 13, 2009, currently only eleven states currently have legislature that supports an enacted twins law." Firstly, these states have passed bills that declare: "No school board shall adopt a policy of automatically separating or placing together twins or other multiples" (3). Second, these bills include a section that states,

> A parent or guardian of twins or other multiples in elementary school may, no later than sixty days before the first day of each school year, request that the twins or multiples be placed in the same classroom or in separate classrooms. This request shall be granted unless the principal, after meeting with the parents and carefully considering the best interest of the children and other children in the school affected by this decision, decides a different placement is necessary (3).

Only two states, Oklahoma and Illinois, have "resolution" meetings allowing parental input. The experts agree that these resolutions are not effective. In some cases, even with a discussion, the children are still placed separately due to "mandatory school policies" (4).

Interestingly, in 1994, Oklahoma was the first state to adopt a resolution calling for school districts to re-think separation practices for twins, allowing   individual situations to be considered (2). Ten states have "sponsored 'twins bills." A sponsored bill means that a member or members of congress 'support' the bill prior to a vote. Ten other states, including California, are awaiting sponsorship. That means, to date, eighteen states have no state policies in place. (see chart – map of US with separate states color coded)

An argument can be made for either side of the coin – separate or keep together. School officials usually agree twins will fail to develop "individuality" unless separated. Nancy Segalm the psychologist who specializes in twin research offers the following retort, a bit tongue and check: "This implies that educators meeting twins for the first time know more about what is best for them than the parents who raised them" (2). Naturally, some twins or multiples will thrive being apart from one another and therefore can be separated while others may suffer from separation anxiety when pulled away from their other twin or siblings. This is similar to how non-twins may have difficulty separating from their parent. The point of enacting legislation is to prevent a "blanket policy." "Clearly a single policy is inappropriate for all twins, just as it is for all non-twins," asserts Nancy Segal (5).

A study was conducted in the Netherlands to determine consequences of classroom separation on twins. They studied and measured the short and long term effects on behavior problems and academic performance. An example of a short term behavioral effect might be acting out where as a long term effect might be depression or a long term sleep disorder problem. The results "suggest that in the long run, for both monozygotic and dizygotic twins, separation does not affect problem behavior or academic achievement." (6)

As our survey shows, Moms and Dads were split down the middle when asked whether or not they separated kids in school. From the interviews I found there seemed to be a slight correlation between choice to separate and gender. If they were GGG triplets they were more often kept together. If they were BBB triplets they were more often separated. Interestingly, was that what worked for some kids one year, didn't necessarily work the next. Fortunately, it seems that parents and educators re-evaluated the choice each year and had an ongoing dialogue about those choices.

· · ·

"The kids were separated in classes at first, but now that they are older it really doesn't matter. I had two in first grade and my son got held back. So, then it was just the girls and up until third grade when they were separated; and then they got put together in a class and they decided that was okay. It was no big deal. Now there's just no problem what-so-ever.

Sports teams were basically the same but they tried to do different things. Tim goes to football, basketball, baseball and the girls did soccer and softball. I have always encouraged them. They are all-three in choir. I would say that my biggest challenge is financial. School trips and things that most people only have to pay for one at a time, I am paying for two with the third right behind them."
   Tracy Ann B., West Jefferson, Ohio, 14 y/o GGB

Twin Laws	Sponsred Twin Bills	Awaiting Sponsorship
Florida	Alabama	California
Georgia	Arizona	Colorado
Louisiana	Arkansas	Connecticut
Massachusetts	Illinois	Idaho
Minnesota	Indiana	North Carolina
New Hampshire	Maryland	Ohio
New Jersey	Michigan	South Dakota
	Missouri	West Virginia
	New York	Wisconsin

"As the girls are just starting kindergarten I have allowed them to stay together, however, I can already see that possible issues may arise in the future requiring there separation in school and activities."
   Sandy L., Alberta, Canada, GGG

Helen kept her kids together in school but on separate teams and in separate art/music classes. "Presently getting through the homework times three teachers, friends, and individual play dates is our biggest challenge."
   Helen K., New York, New York, GGB

Our Survey's Said...

More than half of the parents of multiples in our surveys had children who were not yet old enough to go to school. Out of 228 Questionnaires, only 144 responded. Whether or not parents of multiples split up their children up in school was not convincing one way or another. About 57% said that they did not separate their kids in school while the remaining 43% said they did. These figures do not seem to make a convincing argument either way to say overwhelmingly, "yes" most of the time they are separated or "no" most of the time kids are not.

When personally interviewing parents of multiples, they elaborated more on their answers. Some simply couldn't separate their children in school because in the school district they were in, for example, there were only two classes or, in some cases, only one class. For some, they separated them with one in one class and two in another. While others that had enough classes to separate them individually varied as to whether they chose to separate them at all. It seemed to depend on the age and sex of the children. The pre-kindergarten and kindergarten children were more likely to remain together. The children that were in second grade or higher were more likely to be separated. With regard to sex differences, the parents of multiples who had GGG (girl, girl, girl) triplets, tended to keep them together, while the ones with BBB (boy, boy, boy) triplets, were more likely to separate them.

"Isabel will read a book and go off and do the quiet thing, whereas Sarah and Rachael are almost constantly doing role-playing, you know, "I'm a dog, you're a cat." So they seem so individual that I thought I'd really like to put them in separate classes I felt for so much of their life they were treated as a unit that I really wanted them each to be treated as a person. So, this preschool in the little town we live in had five classes. It was no problem getting them separate classes and, they each love their teacher. They run right in."

Susan A., Cabot, Arkansas, GGG identical

"I love having my kids together in school. They are in 3rd grade and it's easier for us having the same teacher. The kids have always made their own friends; they're never clingy with each other."
Wendie K., BBG

Percent of multiples who were separated in school

If all other responses are filtered out except "yes", "no" and "too young", one can find that out of 228 such responses, 144 (or 56.9%) answered "too young", 48 (or 19%) answered "no", and 36 (or 14.2%) answered "yes". Over half of the triplets covered in this survey are still too young to be in school but among those who are old enough, it seems that their parents are slightly more likely to keep them together in school. A handful of other responses mentioned separating kids on intervals or only split them into 2 groups (2 together and 1 separated).

Bibliography

1. NL Segal, JM Russell. Twins in the classroom: school policy issues and recommendations. Journal of Educational and Psychological Consultation. Vol. 3, No 1. p 69, 1992.

2. NL Segal. Educational issues; twin summaries; famous twin babies and famous twins. Twin Research and Human Genetics. Vol. 8, No 4. pp.409-414, 2005.

3. http://ww.gencourt.state.uh.us/legislation/2007/B0078.html

4. http://www.twinslaw.com

5. NL Segal. Same as separate classrooms: a twin bill; the birth of the

asian society for twin studies; research reviews; more extraordinary live of twins. Twin Research and Human Genetics. Vol. 9, No. 3. pp. 473-8, 2006.

6. M van Leeuwen, SM van den Berg, TCEM van Bejisterveldt, DI Boomsuma. Effects of twin separation in primary school. Twin Research and Human Genetics. Vol. 8, No. 4. pp.384-391, 2005.

Personal Interview
Marci Magnone

CHAPTER NINE

· · · · ·

The Greatest Challenges
Or
Adjusting the Compass

"The biggest challenge is remembering to be a spouse, not just a mother. I get so wrapped up in being a Mom, I forget to make sure my spouse knows how important he is to the family."
   Cindy B., Bear, Deleware, GGB

"We just hate going out. People will stare. There are people who go, 'Oh I would shoot myself if I was you. Oh, I would commit suicide.' Oh, it's like, for the love of God. Really it's rude."

"Why would you say that in front of babies? It gets hurtful. Especially when the people kind of understand what they're talking about. People are idiots."

"I've had one person say to me, 'Are these 'God-given?' Everyone just assumes that you did in-vitro. If you try for so long and you miscarry that many times, people don't know unless they've walked in your shoes."
   Kelli B., Minnesota, GGB

"I try to ask other triplets what they wish their parents had known had they been able to tell them. They say:
   1. Take individual pictures and not just as a group.
   2. Always have individual cakes at birthday time.
   3. Do not ever compare. And
   4. Allow them to be themselves."
   Kerry P., Searcy, Arkansas,BBG

"Our greatest challenge? Balancing the needs of the multiples with the needs of the first born child, how not to have a first born girl over-shadowed by triplet boys. The other biggest challenge is regaining the importance of our marriage as all of the kids grew up."
   Donna C., Williamsville, New York, BBB

"My fifteen-year-old once said to a perfect stranger who came up to our ten month old triplets to take their picture: 'I don't remember you asking my Mom if you could take their pictures?'"
Debbie L., Bonaire, Georgia, GGB, 2 Older girls

Funny Stories

As young children they were extremely mischievous. One summer morning we found the children had decorated the Christmas tree. They somehow managed to bring it out of a very large heavy chest and assemble the whole tree together – it's eight feet high. They must have been around four years at the time and supposed to be asleep in their room. Thankfully, no one was hurt. They looked so pleased with themselves and thought they may have tricked Santa into coming early.
Deborah T., Malta Europe, BBG

The kids love, love, love their bath. As soon as we turn our backs, they're tearing off their clothes and throwing them in the hallway. The other night, my husband was doing the bath; and he turned on the bath went and he went to the kitchen to get something. He turned around and said, "I saw them sittin' in the bathtub, fully clothed, kinda goin' 'Something's not right here.'"
Meredith W. , Lincoln, Nebraska, GGB

When their father, at a quick glance, will call one of our identical boys by name and be ignored. Then he turns to me and says, 'Boy he just doesn't listen does he?' and I get to reply, 'That's because you're talking to James and calling for Christopher.
Julie B., Chillicothe, Ohio, Identical boys (2), fraternal girl (1)

I get a lot of people who say 'I could never do that' or 'I would just die if I had three'. I think that most people underestimate themselves. It's amazing what you can do when you have no choice. I don't think anyone plans on having triplets, but once you have them you just make it happen. Triplets are a blessing and most people I think realize that it is a miracle!
    Kari G., Cedar Rapids, Iowa, GBB Triplets

On Becoming Famous

My primary purpose of writing this book is to de-mystify the world of triplets. I believe that this book may help in this process by revealing the human element of families that have multiples. In essence, I want to attempt to stop the staring, the pointing, and the harsh words that are directed at me, my husband and my beautiful children. I want to protect my children and have them live in a perfectly safe and accepting world where triplets are just like everyone else. I am a mother and I want to do my part to make this world a better place for my children.

I am mesmerized by the 'ideal world of everything equaling two' that I sometimes experience: a world that stays focused on the average family of 2.5 kids and a mini-van family; or a world that gawks at families with three children and wonders "How do they do it?" What messages are my children picking up from this environment? Perhaps telling stories from other parents of multiples will promote more public acceptance of all family sizes.

Peoples' reactions seem universally predictable. If you are having twins they say, "Oh, I always wanted two at once". With triplets its – "Oh my God, you're kidding? …right?" or, "Boy, you'll really have your hands full!" Despite unavoidable ridicule, I was unscathed when I was pregnant with our three. Maybe it was due to the triple shot of super fertility hormones that increased my HCG levels, keeping me either overly relaxed or completely blinded to the future. I kept thinking, three, what a gift. The rose colored glasses I wore showed me a world of optimistic glass-half-full scenarios. Just think, I'd say to myself: "Once I'm done with diapers, I'm done for good" or "They'll all nap together" and, my favorite, "It's just as cheap buying for one as it is for three", and, naturally, "They won't need anything but love and they'll all share each other's company; aren't they lucky?".

Instead of worrying, as I did when I had one child, whether I'm going to arrange enough play dates or if I've plopped him in front of the TV for too long, I am currently concerned about whether or not I am doing what is best for my three kids' psyche. Will they be treated as three precious individuals or judged as one big experiment? It seems everyone has an opinion about – and acceptance seems to depend on – how we got here and whether our children are medical miracles or a rare occurrence of nature.

During their children's infancy while strolling their multiples in their over-priced triplet stroller, most parents are approached by someone who, though well meaning, asks the surprising question, "How did you get them?" or "Are they natural?" Meaning, "Come on, tell me how you did it really…didn't you tamper with old Mother Nature?" They don't want to know if you purchased them at a certain store, or how they can get the same thing, they are just curious.

The same inquisitive person would never walk up to someone walking down the street with a single stroller and ask this, but somehow many outsiders feel that it is perfectly acceptable to ask every triplet parent about the very difficult path of fertility or lack there of it. I used to think they were nosey, but it seems to be a universal question. Parents of multiples need to get thick skin if it bothers them or come up with a creative answer. To the question "Are they natural?" My favorite answer is "No, they are from outer space!"

I've had family members refer to my kids as, "our little experiment". I've also been criticized for "playing with fire" or for "playing God" because we used fertility drugs and IVF. A popular talk show hostess Rosie O'Donnell, recently sponsored a set of identical quadruplets on her show, but she qualified that they were conceived "naturally" as opposed to "other" means, such as artificial insemination. What does it matter if they came to be through fertility drugs, artificial insemination, or alien implantation?

Not everyone loves triplets. For example, we live in Santa Monica, California, not far from the ocean where personal space and square footage have high value and people speak their minds. When someone is pointedly rude to me and my children my feelings are hurt. Maybe I take it too personally and presume they are casting judgment towards my husband and I and our choice to have children with medical support. My fear is that this judgment is going to affect my children and their sense of self and family. I wonder how people would react if they had his same experience. One day, at the crowded coffee shop, that I frequent daily, triplet stroller full of babies in tow, one woman actually said to me: "Can't you park that THING (holding my precious five-month old) outside?" Apparently, it was making it difficult for her to navigate her way around the barista counter with her cell phone in one hand and her latte in the other!

Now, in reality, how would I park my stroller and carry all three babies into the store to get my coffee? Imagine for a minute what that would look like. It is not physically possible. My children and I take up space with or without a stroller. We are allowed to bring it in as there are four of us. Perhaps this lady did not even look in the stroller and was simply annoyed by the very fact of my large stroller being in her way. Maybe she was a childless work-aholic who doesn't understand parenthood. Maybe she was having a bad day. I am not sure, but I do know that this remark deeply hurt and still, five years later bothers me just as much.

Perhaps I am extra sensitive because of all the other remarks and casual comments that people believe they are able to say to me. I guess in the end it is important to remember that there is no accounting for good manners. There will always be people in the world who treat their dogs better than families with more than two kids. I must hold my head high and be confident that I made the right choice for me, not the lady in the coffee shop. If for some odd reason she is reading this book, I would like to say to her that I forgive her for her error in judgement. Make sure you maintain a sense of humor towards other people's lack of good character. Write your story in a journal or share it with someone who understands. At the end of the day, do not carry their rudeness with you; let it go and smile that devilish smile that only we, parents of triplets can really ever know. Life is about giving and sharing together. Our children are our future and that is what really matters.

When asked about funniest thing so far: Well, the new found celebrity feeling you get when you're in public with them all; the stares, the whispers, the questions, the photos. You can't go anywhere quickly (not that you could with triplets any way). It's kind of like you're a freak show, but in a fun way.
Beanie A. - Nurse, Napa, California, GGB

There is not one of my family or friends who envy me! My step-mother feels sorry for me because I don't get out much but I wouldn't have it any other way!
Sara B., Groton, New York, GGB

Do people feel sorry for you or envy you? Probably both – I don't have time to listen to the negative, I only take in the positive. The positive is what keeps me going.
Suzanne C., Avon, Ohio, BBG

Our Surveys Said...

One of the last questions on the survey was "What is the greatest challenge?" Since the question was open-ended many answers were in sentence format or had more than one response. It would be hard to quantify them all, but I've tried to compile what were the most frequent answers and group similar responses together. By now you probably already know my greatest challenges were sleep deprivation and dealing with the public; but these two were not the most popular responses. Hopefully this does not water-down the true meaning of what it is like to be a parent of multiples. As difficult as it was for me to read through them, I certainly could relate to almost every one of the parent's responses. One time or another, over the past five years I have experienced these very same challenges. Some parents have managed better in overcoming them than I have, others have not. This section is not intended to portray the painful parts exclusively but rather present what is most challenging in order to give better perspective to what makes being a parent of multiples different from being a parent of singletons.

Out of 192 responses, the top most frequent answers were:

GREATEST CHALLENGES
1. Being able to give individual attention to all the children in the house (47%).
2. Time, organization and energy to do everything (25%).
3. Sleep, lack of it, or results from sleep deprivation (10%).
4. Managing sibling conflicts or disciplining the children (9%).
5. Finances (9%).
6. Finding time for partner (9%).
7. Dealing with the public or going out in public (8%).
8. Asking for help (5%).
9. Keeping sanity or preventing effects of stress (5%).
10. Carving out time for ones-self (4%).

"I find that these days my biggest challenge is spending quality time with each child. Finding time that is not managing, organizing, preparing or cleaning something or someone seems to be hard to come by. Even when I do find some 'baby time,' I find that I don't have enough arms or lap space to meet all of their needs."
Shelli K., Oswego, Illinois, BBG

1. Spending Alone Time with Each Child Individually

The most frequent response was; "Not being able to spend alone-time with each individual child or with the other sibling(s)." This becomes increasingly difficult if one or more of the children are sick, over-tired or needy in some normal, average, zero-to-five-year-old way. Susan M. from New York said it well: "Giving each girl her share of mommy is the greatest challenge. I want them to grow up as if they were singletons born at the same time." I could easily relate to this, since I had already raised a singleton. Since I knew I couldn't give them each as much individual attention I may have tried to make up for it some how. I recall how angry my husband was when he found out that I bought each of our three their own pedal cars and electronic devices ("Leapsters"), for example. Perhaps they didn't need such individual purchases, especially since a regular box is much more fun to play in. Sharing seems intuitive for them, but it was foreign to me.

When our children were infants it was extremely difficult to spend enough one-on-one, individual time with them. My older son definitely took a back seat to the needs of the three, especially since our three had been in and out of the hospital. CW agreed, "The challenge is maintaining a healthy relationship with the older child while raising three infants." Even if there is not an older or younger sibling keeping healthy relationships with children takes time and there are only so many hours in the day. Amy P. from Indianapolis, Indiana agrees, "Splitting time amongst the three kids is difficult." Keeping this in perspective may make it easier when and if someone offers to help out. Being able to just take one with you to the market for some "Mommy time," may be enough to pacify your Mommy guilt. Other suggestions from parents of multiples are to alternate weekend outings with the kids because often times both parents are home and therefore more available to help out. Our kids always remember our special days with them. I have one visitor who comes for a week every year and she and I take out one child a day with us to the zoo, park or the dinosaur museum and they love it.

As our kids grew to preschool age, the individual demands were less and the kids surprised me. What I didn't expect was that they would actually need less of me during this time period, because these toddlers had something my singleton never had – built-in playmates. In fact, with my one child I remember feeling the struggle of having to be his sole source of entertainment. That sort of Mommy guilt didn't exist with the three of them, because they all played together.

Now as our three are five going on six I see them needing more individual time with us. They talk over one another in order to get my attention. As they get older, their skill sets change and some may be good readers, while others may be good at math or sports. Laura B. from Willow Springs, Illinois, put it well, "Our greatest challenge is trying to let each one know they are special in their own way." I tell people, they are all born on the same day, but they are all different and unique in their own way. They don't necessarily all like to do the same activities or to hang out with the same friends. In that sense they are very much like singletons, just ones that were born on the same day.

"Do whatever works. My husband is not a 'baby/infant' person. No matter how hard I tried to get him to feed/change, etc., it just wasn't happening. We were wasting too much energy arguing about him not helping with the babies. What worked for us was him basically doing EVERYTHING else. (I didn't even put wipes in the wipe container or get gas in my car) his part was keeping the house together, shopping, etc., doing things with our older son (five years old at the time) and I

did the triplets probably for over a year and believe it or not it worked."
   Mary S., White Haven, Pennsylvania, BBG

2. Finding Enough Time, Organization and Energy to Do Everything

*"My biggest challenge is that I can't go to the grocery store when-
ever I want to; I have to wait for someone to get home."*
   Shelley B., Comanche, Texas, BBG

The next most fashionable challenge was organization. It's true as one Mom said; "Every time we go somewhere it looks like we're planning a trip to Europe." Nearly everyone agreed not only was there not enough "time" to get everything done, but also there wasn't enough "preparedness" to feel like one is ready for anything that might come along. Dr. Seuss must have known many families of multiples when he gave this piece of advice in Oh the Places You'll Go; "Be sure when you step, step with care and great tact and remember that Life's a Great Balancing Act." (3)

Another section of the questionnaire asked if the parents had any advice for other parents of multiples. In this section a recurrent piece of advice was "Get a schedule and stick to it." It's all about trying to stay one-and-a-half steps ahead if possible. That means knowing what's for dinner a day in advance because there will be no running out to the store when home alone with three little ones all day. This was especially hard for me since I didn't major in home economics like my mother-in-law. A few Moms suggested a cookbook called Saving Dinners. (2) This cook book outlines weekly meal plans including a shopping list for all of the items. (Something you could even read to your husband before he heads home from work! That saves a great deal of car-seat to grocery transfer!)

Another interesting suggestion was a nationwide company called, "Dream Dinners." You prepare meals in their kitchen facilities that you can put in the freezer for the up-coming month. No shopping on your part involved.

Besides meal preparation, there's everyday up-keep of the house and all of the other domestic duties such as sorting out toys and clothes that they have outgrown.   RK says her challenge is "finding the most efficient way of doing things." Every minute counts. With our kids, we try to read to them every night for fifteen minutes, one book a piece. But some nights we are just too tired. Michelle A. from Dacula, Georgia, says her challenge is "Having time to read to them everyday and scheduling." The best advice I heard so far for getting their kids to read on their own was a mom of multiples who said she let her son play fifteen minutes of video games for every fifteen minutes he read to his two sisters out loud. Maybe, if there's not enough time in the day to read to the kids your self, having them read to each other is just as beneficial. Never underestimate the bond they share together and their willingness to cooperate with one another. As far as having enough time, energy and organization to make it through the long days, many parents commented that they were able to do more than they had expected of themselves. They felt this extra boost stemmed from having three who needed them to "be there" for them. Some even commented that having three forced them to focus more and get organized sooner than when they had only one.

3. Other Challenges

"I found that you have to have a 'go with the flow' kind of attitude with three babies around! Things come up that you weren't expecting and you can't let those things throw you off course. Jason and I found that the more we just go with the flow, the better things seem to run and we don't get too stressed about little things. Life always goes on.

That being said..we always worry about finances. Children are expensive and with triplets there's pretty much three times the expense. It has, however, taught us to be a little more money savvy and take every expense into consideration."

Kally K., GGG

The next most frequent answers were not as common as the first two: sleep deprivation, finances, time with your partner, dealing with the public, staying sane, asking for help and carving out "me" time. No surprise these topics have been presented in previous chapters. With each challenge as parents we strive to live and learn to make it better for the next time. Any parent whether they have one child or ten, has all these challenges except for maybe having to deal with the public and their nosy questions. This is why I addressed this at the beginning of this chapter. Heather F from Rochester, New York, reminded me how important it is to "Help the outside world see them as individuals." She went on to comment how she tries to "Give her three experiences outside of the house that are not just show and tell for strangers." Parents of singletons don't have to worry so much about having to explain them selves to strangers.

The theme, "Staying sane" was reiterated in the comments section under greatest challenges. Topics included post partum depression, new parent concerns of "having no direction," to "making sure they are healthy and happy." These stresses are present in all parents but may be multiplied to some degree when the work load is compounded. Gretchen G. from Swedesboro, New Jersey, quoted my husband's all time favorite movie: "I don't know if you've seen the move 'Groundhog Day' [with Bill Murray], but every morning seems like that movie." In the movie, Bill Murray wakes up to the same day over and over again for what seems like years. Gretchen adds, "Getting any break from being 'on,' is our greatest challenge. We are completely blessed and ecstatic however, we are never 'caught up' on anything."

The stress of day in and day out makes it difficult to take time away to be with your partner or to be alone. It probably is easier, and certainly less expensive, to get a baby sitter for one child versus three. Many parents commented how they wished they could have spent a little more time away together. Some parents had creative solutions to this. Heather K. from Cincinnati, Ohio with GGG triplets said: "Our daughters have three sets of grandparents (my parents are divorced and remarried).

About every six weeks, we separate the girls and they spend the weekend with a set of grandparents. It gives the girls individualized attention and the grandparents love having them over all to themselves for the weekend. Plus, it gives Adam and I a weekend to focus on just us and rekindle our marriage."

If I learned anything from talking with so many generous parents it's to value and respect each other as much as possible and make time for each other when possible. Our children learn by example and can only treat others how they see us interact together.

"The second greatest challenge for us was making our marriage work. It was hard to find time for ourselves. The first biggest challenge was treating our kids as three separate kids as much as possible. Take time to nurture your relationship with your partner. This is difficult, but so important as the kids get older."

Amy F., Lancaster, Pennsylvania, GGB

Discipline and Managing Sibling Rivalry

We live in an older home with a forced air heating system. When the trips were 2, they took the cover off the cold-air returns and climbed in!

Jackie K., Preschool teacher, Lakewood, Ohio, BBG

My 8 y/o daughter wasn't supposed to take stuffed animals to school and we got into the habit of 'patting her down'. So, she hid her animal under her winter hat.

Margie S., Sykesville, Pennsylvania, GGB

"Year one is the year of no sleep and five is the year of fighting," one parent of multiples said. I had to agree; parents of multiples seem to find the kindergarten year, usually age five, the year of challenge and conflict amongst siblings. Perhaps it is because their view of themselves is changing as they now have a peer group to compare themselves to. This year is a year of establishing themselves as independent in the family and the world.

This is a year of immense growth for multiples especially as they are often treated as a group. For them it is even more of a challenge to establish an identity in the midst of brothers and sisters – especially if they look alike. Many parents gave the advice: "Go with the flow and don't let bumps in the road get you down;" but when fighting leads to destruction of property and hurt feelings, it's tough to "go with it." Boundaries and limits need to be set and a fair amount of police work is in order at times. My good friend, Diana, has two that are about eighteen months apart who has two boys who love and respect each other very much, because they are given an appropriate amount of boundaries. She is an amazing Mom. Her husband had to take over while she was gone for the day and her advice to him was: "If it's a day that ends in a 'Y' there's going to be crying, tantruming, timing out, counting and someone's going to lose a toy."

My brother and his wife sent us a "Chore chart" when the kids turned around four or five. At first I thought it was sort of a "hint." Was he gently trying to tell me to start disciplining my kids? I realized he was just passing down something he felt might help us as he himself had found it helpful with his children. The truth is we did start a chore chart, we just "triplet-proofed" it. It did work; although not necessarily on the chart-our kids took all the stickers off and placed the reward stars all over their room for decorations!

We use the "dime" jar philosophy from "Nanny 911." For my first son Tim, it was a quarter jar, but with the current economy, dimes will have to do. Every day our three five-year-olds have certain chores they have to do themselves: get dressed, brush their teeth, and comb their hair, (my daughter never earns her dime for this one!).

We add things we want them to do such as, "Do something nice for your other siblings" or "Pick up after your self." It can be used as a positive and negative reinforcement. If our teenager says a cuss word and the triplets catch him, he has to add a dime to the dime jar, and if they repeat the word, we take a dime out. It seems to work for now, but I'm sure the bar will have to be raised when they get older.

Setting boundaries is no different in a household with one or three kids. It may be more difficult to enforce when parents are "outnumbered." But, most parents find once structure is in place, a calmer household follows. Cindy L. from Chicago with GGB triplets says "Discipline is a problem. I am 'outnumbered!' Around the house they get into things they shouldn't. They do listen better to their father when he gets home." It drives me crazy when our kids do exactly what they are told by their teachers and yet won't do the simplest thing I ask them to do. But I always keep in mind that our kids' teachers usually are managing twenty other children at the same time so for them perhaps it's easier to be consistent because they have them for a short time, like the father who comes home and is more effective at the end of the day.

What is different is that with three at a time on the same developmental track it's hard not to compare them to their peers. Rachel P. from New Zealand said for her the "Challenge was the competition of the three of them comparing each amongst themselves." One Mom explained how her kids were all on the swim team but each one did different events. That way, during the meets each one took turns on the sidelines cheering their other siblings on rather than competing against them. They chose the different events and had invaluable experiences in sports because of the separation.

CONCLUSION
Summary chart of yes/no questions asked on the survey

Question:	Percentage who answered "Yes"	Number of Responses recieved
Any trouble getting pregnant?	78	245
Were you asked to reduce?	64	227
Put on bed rest?	75	243
Did you breast feed?	65	243
Did you sleep train?	47	
Any back pain in pregnancy?	66	243
Did you participate in exercise Group?	33	240
Have you lost your baby weight	64	241
Did family come and help?	81	177
Did you hire day help?	27	177
Did you hire night help?	16	177
Did you separate kids in classes?	43	144

Whatever the challenges, the benefits far outweigh the struggles. The joy of watching our family grow to accept and respect each other and share the journey together is priceless. As I look back on the advice from other parents I hope to alleviate some worry for other expecting parents or demystify for those who have not experienced this journey.

Next time someone is walking with a triplet stroller keep in mind there is a good chance that person had a difficult time conceiving and she may not want to discuss the intimate details of how she did it. Also, try not to ask the parents why they did or did not reduce; it is a sensitive issue, not public record. As parents of multiples ignore any rude comments and prepare for curious on-looking.

If you are pregnant with multiples keep in mind you will probably go on bed-rest, and some of the time it will be at the hospital. Take the doctor's recommendations on bed-rest seriously and try to get specifics. Weight gain with more than one is higher, but weight loss after the birth happens two-thirds of the time. The weight loss may take nine months, so why not incorporate strolling with the kids into your daily routine? The incidence of back pain will not be any greater if you are carrying more than one.

Feel confident that more often than not moms of multiples breast-feed for as long as singleton moms do. It may mean being a little more creative such as pumping or alternating, but chances are milk production will not be the limiting factor. Sleep may be the bigger problem. Only about half of the moms surveyed initiated a regimented sleep training schedule. Think about this carefully and talk with other parents of multiples when making a decision.

As the children develop and grow, try to take as many pictures as possible, not just of all three together, but of each one individually. Respect their differences. There won't be time for everything, so prioritize. Make time for your partner as much as possible. Don't be ashamed to ask for help and when it is offered, humbly accept. In our surveys family pitched in to help more than hired outside help. If possible try to talk to other friends who have multiples to get advice from them. Whether you separate them in school classes or keep them together, it is a balancing act. Our children teach us the trade, if we put the time into learning their skills. Let them teach you how to juggle, they've been doing it since they were in the womb together. Life is a great balancing act, and three is a magic number!

Favorite Books for Parents of Multiples, Selected by Parents of Multiples

Here is a list of favorite books for parents of multiples and their children. This list was collected from the 250 surveys we received. They are in alphabetical order rather than order of popularity. The two most frequently recommended books were <u>When You're Expecting Twins, Triplets, or Quads</u> by Dr. Barbara Luke and <u>You're all my Favorites</u> by Sam McBratney.

1. <u>Dr. Spock's Baby and Child Care: 8th Edition</u> by Benjamin Spock
2. <u>Exceptional Pregnancies. A Survival Guide to Parents Expecting Triplets or More</u> by Kathleen Birch and Janet Bleyl
3. <u>Flicka, Ricka, and Dicka</u> (series) by Maj Lindman
4. <u>I Sleep at Red Lights: A True Story of Life After Triplets</u> by Bruce Stockler
5. <u>Healthy Sleep Habits, Happy Child</u> by Marc Weissbluth
6. <u>I Can't Wait to Meet You</u> by Claudia Santorelli- Bates
7. <u>Kids are Worth It</u> by Barbara Coloroso
8. <u>Make Way for Triplets</u> by Fran Bevington and Dan Bevington
9. <u>Mothering Multiples: Breastfeeding and Caring for Twins or More!</u> by Karen Kerkhoff Gromada
10. <u>Multiple Blessings. Surviving and Thriving with Twins and Sextuplets</u> by Kate and Jon Gosselin and Beth Carson
11. <u>On Becoming</u> Babywise by Gary Ezzo
12. <u>Pea Pod Babies</u> by Karen Baicker and Sam Williams
13. <u>Raising Multiple Birth Children: A Parent's Survival Guide, Birth-Age 3</u> by William Laut
14. <u>Secrets of the Baby Whisperer: How to Calm, Connect, and Communicate with Your Baby</u> by Tracy Hogg and Melinda Blau
15. <u>Snip, Snap, and Snurr</u> (series) by Maj Lindman
16. <u>Snuggle Bunnies</u> by Lisa McCue
17. <u>The Day the Babies Crawled Away</u> by Peggy Rathmann

18. <u>The Everything Twins, Triplets, And More Book: From Seeing The First Sonogram To Coordinating Nap Times And Feedings – All You Need To Enjoy Your Multiples (Everything: Parenting and Family)</u> by Pamela Fierro
19. <u>TripleFun: From Infertility to Triplets</u> by Lia Shackelford
20. <u>Triplets Go Camping: Triplets Series</u> by Mercé Company Gonzáles
21. <u>The Multiples Manual: Preparing and Caring for Twins or Triplets</u> by Lynn Lorenz and Shelley Dieterichs
22. <u>The Multiple Pregnancy Sourcebook: Pregnancy and the First Days with Twins, Triplets, and More</u> by Nancy A. Bowers
23. <u>The New Contented Little Baby Book: The Secret to Calm and Confident Parenting</u> by Gina Ford
24. <u>When You're Expecting Twins, Triplets, and More: A Doctor's Guide to a Healthy and Happy Multiple Pregnancy</u> by Rachel McClintock Franklin
25. <u>When You're Expecting Twins, Triplets, or Quads</u> by Dr. Barbara Luke
26. <u>You're all my Favorites</u> by Sam McBratney

Glossary of Terms

ART – Assisted reproductive technologies, includes in vitro fertilization (IVF), gamete intrafallopian transfer (GIFT), and intracytoplasmic sperm injection (ICSI), among others. ART procedures involve removing eggs from the woman's ovaries and placing them with sperm. Most procedures occur in the lab and then the embryos are placed in the woman'ts fallopian tube or uterus.

Cerclage: Cervical cerclage (tracheloplasty), also known as a cervical stitch, is used for the treatment of cervical incompetence (or insufficiency),a condition where the cervix has become slightly open and there is a risk of miscarriage because it may not remain closed throughout pregnancy.

Fetus - terms used for an unborn baby starting from 9 weeks gestations to birth.

FSH – Follicle-stimulating hormone regulates the development, growth, pubertal maturation, and reproductive processes of the body. FSH and Luteinizing hormone (LH) act synergistically in reproduction.
Introitus: Another name for the vaginal orifice.

IUI or Intra-uterine insemination - the process by which sperm is placed into the reproductive tract of a woman for the purpose of impregnating her by using means other than sexual intercourse.
It is a form of assisted reproductive technology, used to primarily treat infertility .This procedure may be used when there is low sperm count, decreased sperm mobility, hostile cervical condition (thick mucus), sexual dysfunction, or when a donor sperm is required.

IVF or In vitro fertilization - is a process by which egg cells are fertilised by sperm outside the womb, in vitro. IVF is a major treatment in <u>infertility</u> when other methods of <u>assisted reproductive technology</u> have failed. The process involves hormonally controlling the ovulatory process, removing <u>ova</u> (eggs) from the woman's <u>ovaries</u> and letting <u>sperm</u> fertilise them in a fluid medium. The fertilised egg (<u>zygote</u>) is then transferred to the patient's <u>uterus</u> with the intent to establish a successful pregnancy.

PCOS - Polycystic ovary syndrome is one of the most common female endocrine disorders affecting approximately 5%-10% of women of reproductive age (12-45years old) and is one of the leading causes of <u>infertility</u>.

Peri-natalogist - an obstetrician with specific credentials for managing high-risk pregnancies.

Pre-eclampsia –a sudden increase in blood pressure or pregnancy induced hypertension with significant amounts of protein in the urine, usually after the 20th week of pregnancy.

Selective Reduction - abortion of one or more but not all embryos in a pregnancy with multiple embryos.

TED hose - severely tight stockings that you wear on your legs to prevent blood clots. They are usually worn by patients in the hospital who are bedridden and not able to get up and move around a lot.

Reproductive endocrinologist - A reproductive endocrinologist is a type of medical doctor who specializes in treating people with reproductive disorders.

Thank you to the following families/photographers for contributing their pictures.

Cover: Wilnerd Family – Paige, Cade and Kira – Cassey Fritton Photography, www.frittonphoto.com

Chapter One: Kocke Family – Amy Drouet Photography

Chapter Two: Holderness Family – personal photo

Chapter Three: Campbell Family – Abe Clary Photographer

Chapter Four: Bahr Family – personal photo

Chapter Five: Laurento Family – personal photo

Chapter Six: Gala Family – personal photo

Chapter Seven: Corley Family – personal photo

Chapter Eight: Gala Family – personal photo

Chapter Nine: Crowder Family – Christine Bentley Photographer